W9-CRP-342

Thesaurus of Scales and Melodic Patterns

Nicolas Slonimsky

Amsco Publications
New York/London/Paris/Sydney

Copyright 1947 Charles Scribner's Sons
Copyright renewed 1975 by Charles Scribner's Sons

All rights reserved. No part of this book may be
reproduced or transmitted in any form or by any means,
electronic or mechanical, including photocopying, recording,
or by any information storage and retrieval system,
without permission in writing from the Publisher.

SCHIRMER BOOKS
A Division of Macmillan Publishing Co., Inc.
866 Third Avenue, New York NY10022

Collier Macmillan Canada, Ltd.

This Edition is reprinted by arrangement with Schirmer Books.
Exclusive distributors to the Music Trade
in the United States and Canada under licence from
Schirmer Books, A Division of Macmillan Publishing Co., Inc.
Music Sales Corporation
180 Madison Avenue, 24th Floor,
New York, NY10016 USA.

Library of Congress Catalog Card Number: 86-75442

Library of Congress Catalog-in-Publication Data

Slonimsky, Nicolas, 1894-
    Thesaurus of scales and melodic patterns.
    Previously published: New York: C Scribner, 1947.
    1. Musical intervals and scales.   I. Title
MT45.S55   1986   86-75442
ISBN 0-02-611850-5

Printed in Great Britain

CONTENTS

THESAURUS OF SCALES AND MELODIC PATTERNS

INTRODUCTION

THE PRESENT THESAURUS is a reference book of scales and melodic patterns, analogous in function with phrase books and dictionaries of idiomatic expressions. But while phrase books are limited to locutions consecrated by usage, the THESAURUS includes a great number of melodically plausible patterns that are new. In fact, many compositions appearing in recent years contain thematic figures identical with those found in the THESAURUS.

From time to time musical theorists have suggested the possibility of forming entirely new scales based on the division of the octave into several equal parts. As early as 1911 the Italian musician Domenico Alaleona proposed such new scales. Alois Haba, in his *Neue Harmonielehre* (1927), classifies a great number of scales based on equal intervals and suggests harmonizations of these new scales. Joseph Schillinger in his posthumously published *Schillinger System of Musical Composition* classifies new tonal progressions in the chapter Theory of Pitch-Scales.

The scales and melodic patterns in the THESAURUS are systematized in a manner convenient to composers in search of new materials. The title THESAURUS OF SCALES AND MELODIC PATTERNS is chosen advisedly. The term scale, as here used, means a progression, either diatonic or chromatic, that proceeds uniformly in one direction, ascending or descending, until the terminal point is reached. A melodic pattern, on the other hand, may be formed by any group of notes that has melodic plausibility. There are scales of 4 notes only; and there are scales and patterns of 12 different notes. But counting repeated notes appearing in different octaves, a scale may have as many as 48 functionally different notes, as in the Disjunct Major Polytetrachord (No. 958). As to melodic patterns, there is virtually no limit to the number of such tones.

The THESAURUS is arranged in the form of piano scales and melodic studies. No fingering is given, for the pianist will readily find the type of digitation best suited to the hand. Other instrumentalists, too, will find most of the scales and melodic patterns in the THESAURUS adaptable to their instruments. The notation throughout is enharmonic, and accidentals are used according to convenience. Double sharps and double flats are avoided entirely. Precautionary natural signs are placed here and there when an unusual melodic interval occurs. All accidentals affect only the note immediately following.

The scales and patterns in the THESAURUS are arranged according to the principal interval of each particular section. In order to avoid association with a definite tonality, these basic intervals are here referred to by Latin and Greek names derived from old usage. In addition, new terms had to be coined for intervals not in the system of historic scales. In these new terms the prefix *sesqui* stands for the addition of one-half of a tone. Thus, Sesquitone is 1½ tones, or a minor third; Sesquiquadritone is 4½ tones, or a major sixth; and Sesquiquinquetone is 5½ tones, or a major seventh.

The table of intervals from the semitone to the major seventh appears as follows:

Semitone	Minor Second	*Tritone*	Augmented Fourth
Whole Tone	Major Second	*Diapente*	Perfect Fifth
Sesquitone	Minor Third	*Quadritone*	Minor Sixth
Ditone	Major Third	*Sesquiquadritone*	Major Sixth
Diatessaron	Perfect Fourth	*Quinquetone*	Minor Seventh
	Sesquiquinquetone	Major Seventh	

The interval of a major ninth is called Septitone, to indicate that it contains 7 whole tones.

These basic intervals are regarded as fractions of one or more octaves. Thus, the Tritone Progression represents the division of the octave into 2 equal parts, and it produces sequential scales and patterns. The Ditone Progression is the division of the octave into 3 equal parts, and is intervallically identical with the augmented triad. The Sesquitone Progression is the division of the octave into 4 equal parts, and is identical with the familiar diminished-seventh chord. The Whole-Tone scale represents the equal division of the octave into 6 parts. The Semitone Progression is equivalent to the chromatic scale. By the process of permutation the chromatic scale is productive of characteristic patterns of the 12-tone technique.

By dividing 2 octaves into 3 equal parts we obtain the Quadritone Progression, which is closely related to the Ditone Progression, being in fact a spread-out augmented triad. By dividing 3 octaves into 4 equal parts we obtain the interval of the major sixth. This is the Sesquiquadritone Progression, which is an unfolded Sesquitone Progression, productive of patterns related to diminished-seventh harmonies.

In the cycle of scales the interval of a perfect fifth is one-twelfth part of 7 octaves, and it is so represented in the Diapente Progression. A perfect fourth is one-twelfth part of 5 octaves, and is classified as such in the section Diatessaron Progression.

Pursuing a similar process, we find that the Sesquiquinquetone Progression, or the progression of major sevenths, is the result of the equal division of 11 octaves into 12 parts. Finally, the Septitone Progression is the equal division of 7 octaves into 6 parts, with the basic interval of a major ninth.

Scales and melodic patterns are formed by the processes of Interpolation, Infrapolation, and Ultrapolation. The word Interpolation is in common usage; here it signifies the insertion of one or several notes between the principal tones. Infrapolation and Ultrapolation are coined words. Infrapolation indicates the addition of a note below a principal tone; Ultrapolation is the addition of a note above the next principal tone. Infrapolation and Ultrapolation result in the shift of direction, with the melodic line progressing in zigzags. Infrapolation, Interpolation and Ultrapolation may be freely combined, resulting in hyphenated forms: Infra-Interpolation, Infra-Ultrapolation, and Infra-Inter-Ultrapolation.

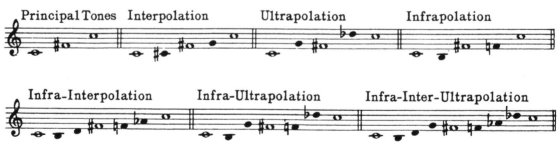

ii

Progressions and patterns based on unequal division of the octave are exemplified by Heptatonic scales and Pentatonic scales. Among Heptatonic scales, or 7-tone scales, are our familiar major and minor scales as well as the church modes. In the section Heptatonic Arpeggios the scales are spread out in thirds. In the section Bitonal Arpeggios the C major arpeggio is combined with arpeggios in all other 23 major and minor keys.

Busoni, who had earnestly explored new musical resources, found 113 different scales of 7 notes. Mentioning as an example the scale: C, Db, Eb, Fb, Gb, Ab, Bb, C (it is No. 1035 in the THESAURUS), he writes in his *Entwurf einer neuen Aesthetik der Tonkunst:* "There is a significant difference between the sound of this new scale when C is taken as the tonic and when it is taken as the leading tone of the scale of Db minor. By harmonizing the tonic with the customary C major triad as a fundamental chord, a novel harmonic sensation is obtained."

In his *Chronicle of My Musical Life* Rimsky-Korsakov mentions the use he made of an 8-tone scale, formed by alternating major and minor seconds. This is Scale No. 393 in the THESAURUS. Sporadic uses of the Whole-Tone scale are found in Glinka and even in Mozart (as a jest to mock the inept *Dorfmusikanten*), but it did not become a deliberate device before Debussy. In Debussy's piano piece *Voiles* the principal melodic structure is in the Whole-Tone scale, but the middle part is written exclusively on the black keys, exemplifying the Pentatonic scale.

The Whole-Tone scale has 6 notes to the octave; the Pentatonic scale has five. The Whole-Tone scale is possible in only one form on a given note, but there can be many Pentatonic scales. There are 49 Pentatonic scales in the THESAURUS.

The 12-Tone Technique of composition promulgated by Schoenberg is based on permutations of the Semitone scale. Various 12-tone patterns are found in the THESAURUS in examples No. 1214 to No. 1318. For example, it is possible to arrange the 12 chromatic tones in 2 major and 2 minor triads without repeating a note. It is also possible to form 4 mutually exclusive augmented triads using all 12 chromatic tones. The theme of Liszt's *Faust* Symphony is composed of 4 augmented triads. It is further possible to split the chromatic scale into a diminished triad, a minor triad, a major triad, and an augmented triad. These mutually exclusive triads can be arranged in the form of Quadritonal Arpeggios.

A recent development of the 12-Tone Technique is the 11-interval technique, which prescribes the formation of progressions containing 11 different intervals. The idea was first introduced by the Austrian musician Fritz Klein in 1921 in a curious composition entitled *Die Maschine,* with the sub-title *Ex-Tonal Self-Satire.* The name of the composer was concealed behind a characteristic nom de plume *Heautontimorumenus* which means Self-Torturer. In this piece Klein introduced a Mother Chord which contains not only all 11 different intervals, but 12 different notes as well.

A further elaboration on the Mother Chord is an invertible 11-interval, 12-tone chord introduced by the author and appropriately christened Grandmother Chord. It has all the intervallic properties of the Mother Chord plus an especial order of intervals so arranged that they are alternately odd-numbered and even-numbered when counted in semitones, with the row of odd-numbered intervals forming a decreasing arithmetical progression and the row of even-numbered intervals forming an increasing arithmetical progression. The order of notes in the Grandmother Chord is identical with the 12-tone Spiral Pattern No. 1232a.

iii

All chords composed of 11 different intervals add up to the interval of 66 semitones, which is the sum of the arithmetical progression from 1 to 11. The interval of 66 semitones equals 5½ octaves, and so forms a Tritone between the lowest and the highest tones in the Pyramid Chord, Mother Chord, Grandmother Chord, and other 11-interval structures.

Scales and patterns listed in the main body of the THESAURUS readily lend themselves to new melodic possibilities. For instance, a descending scale may be played in the form of the melodic inversion of the ascending scale, as suggested in the section Mirror Interval Progressions. It is possible to form complementary scales in the range of 2 octaves, by using in the second octave the notes not used in the first. Other possibilities for the formation of new patterns are demonstrated in the section on Permutations.

A Diatonic counterpart of the 12-Tone Technique is the system of Pandiatonic composition. The term Pandiatonic, first introduced by this writer in 1937, denotes the free use of all 7 tones of the diatonic scale, both melodically and harmonically. In one-part Pandiatonic Progressions, the melody is made up of 7 different notes of the diatonic scale. Such a progression may then be melodically inverted, read backward, or both, resulting in 4 different forms. Pandiatonic Counterpoint in strict style uses progressions of 7 different notes in each voice, with no vertical duplication.

Pandiatonic Harmony is the twentieth century counterpart of classical harmony. Modern composers of such varied backgrounds and musical persuasions as Ravel, Stravinsky, Hindemith, Milhaud, Copland and Roy Harris make use of this technique, arriving at it by different creative processes. Jazz composers, too, have found, by sheer experimentation, effective application for the enriched chords of Pandiatonic formations. It is a common practice to end an orchestral arrangement of a popular song by the enriched major triad with an added sixth, seventh, or ninth.

The concluding sections of the THESAURUS demonstrate the various methods by which tonal materials may be used to best advantage. The section Double Notes shows the combinations derived from corresponding scales and patterns. Plural Scales and Arpeggios give examples of common major and minor progressions arranged consecutively in chromatic transposition. Polytonal Scales are simultaneous progressions in different keys. Polyrhythmic Scales are progressions in different rhythms. Polytonal Polyrhythmic Scales combine different rhythms in different tonalities.

A special word is to be said about Palindromic Canons. Palindromes are words or sentences that read the same forward or backward, as the sentence *Able Was I Ere I Saw Elba* (applied to Napoleon). Similarly, Palindromic Canons read the same backward or forward. The two Palindromic Canons based on Pattern No. 72 are particularly interesting. They result in a progression of enharmonic triads or their inversions, alternating in major and minor keys.

Fragments of the scales and patterns in the THESAURUS may be used as motives and themes. The rhythmical elaboration is left to the imagination of the composer. By using a portion of a pattern in forward and retrograde motion, in varied rhythms within a given meter, it is possible to form an unlimited number of melodic figures.

Rhythmic Development

Pattern №194

Two formulas are used in the harmonization of the scales and patterns: one by common triads, and one by seventh-chords. In the harmonization by common triads, only root positions of major triads in close harmony are applied. Either the root, the third, or the fifth may appear in the melody. These positions are referred to as Octave, Tertian, and Quintan, or in figures, 8, 3, and 5. When the melody ascends, diatonically or chromatically, the positions change from the Octave to the Tertian to the Quintan to the Octave. When the melody descends, the order of the positions is reversed. Furthermore, the order of positions may be reversed at the end of a cadence even in ascending motion. When the melody is stationary, the order of positions is free. The resulting harmony traverses several tonalities in an alternation of successive major chords.

Harmonization in Major Triads
(Figures Indicate Intervals Between the Melody and the Bass)

The harmonization in major triads is found in the music of Debussy, Moussorgsky, and other composers of the French and Russian schools. A classical example is the scene in the monk's cell in Moussorgsky's opera *Boris Godunov*. In the second act of Puccini's opera *Tosca* the Whole-Tone scale in the bass is harmonized by a row of major triads with the positions following the Octave-Tertian-Quintan (8-3-5) formula.

Moussorgsky: *Boris Godunov*   Puccini: *Tosca* (Whole-Tone Scale in the Bass)

The second type of harmonization is effected by means of Master Chords. These Master Chords are dominant-seventh chords with the fifth omitted. In combination with melodic elements of a given scale or pattern, these chords form harmonic structures of the type of seventh-chords, ninth-chords, or whole-tone chords. The Master Chords are indicated for ascending scales and patterns in the sections Tritone Progression, Ditone Progression and Sesquitone Progression by figures within circles, as ⑤, and are used to harmonize an entire rhythmic group in a given progression. In the Tritone and Sesquitone Progressions it is also possible to harmonize the entire octave range with a single Master Chord. Furthermore, any Master Chord suitable for harmonization of a given progression may be transposed a tritone up or down with satisfactory results.

Harmonization with Master Chords

Pattern № 53   Pattern № 186   Pattern № 393

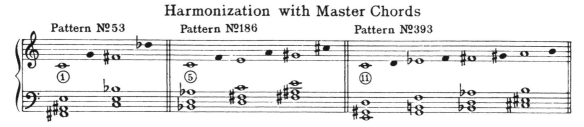

Harmonization of both types is given in the tables on pp.240-241. To harmonize in major triads, it is necessary to alternate the Octave, Tertian, and Quintan positions given in the table. In harmonizing by seventh-chords, ninth-chords, and whole-tone chords, any chord under a given melody note will furnish a workable harmony.

The patterns in the Diatessaron and Diapente Progressions lend themselves to harmonization characteristic of the Dominant-Tonic cycle. When harmonized in consecutive seventh-chords, such patterns acquire a Schumannesque quality.

Harmonization in Seventh-Chords

A harmonization of the Dominant-Tonic type will impart a feeling of tonality even to a 12-tone progression.

Tonal Harmonization of a 12-Tone Pattern

Traditional harmonization in major and minor keys uses chords formed by the diatonic scale. Similarly, new scales may be harmonized with the aid of chords formed by the notes of the scale itself. Examples of such Autochordal Harmonization are given in a special table. There are scales that admit of only 2 different triads, as Scale No. 7, which can be harmonized with C major and F♯ major triads. The 8-tone scale No. 393 is capable of forming 8 different triads, while other scales, such as No. 5, do not yield a single triad.

All scales and patterns in the THESAURUS are centered on C as the initial and concluding tone. It goes without saying that these progressions can be transposed to any tonal center according to a composer's requirements.

John Stuart Mill once wrote: "I was seriously tormented by the thought of the exhaustibility of musical combinations. The octave consists only of five tones and two semitones, which can be put together in only a limited number of ways of which but a small proportion are beautiful: most of these, it seemed to me, must have been already discovered, and there could not be room for a long succession of Mozarts and Webers to strike out, as these have done, entirely new surpassing rich veins of musical beauty. This sort of anxiety, may, perhaps, be thought to resemble that of the philosophers of Laputa, who feared lest the sun be burnt out."

The fears of John Stuart Mill are unjustified. There are 479,001,600 possible combinations of the 12 tones of the chromatic scale. With rhythmic variety added to the unbounded universe of melodic patterns, there is no likelihood that new music will die of internal starvation in the next 1000 years.

NICOLAS SLONIMSKY

1 January 1947 Boston, Massachusetts

EXPLANATION OF TERMS

AUTOCHORDAL HARMONIZATION. Application of chords derived from the tones of a given scale (Example, Scale No. 12: C, D♯, F, F♯, A, B, C, harmonized in 2 triads, F major and B major).

BITONAL ARPEGGIOS. [Nos. 1191-1213]. Melodic progressions formed of alternating arpeggios in 2 different keys.

BITONAL PALINDROMIC CANONS. Canons that result in the formation of 6-tone chords composed of 2 triads (Example, Scale No. 7: C, C♯, E, F♯, G, A♯, C, developed canonically, forming bitonal chords of C major and F♯ major).

CHORD OF THE MINOR 23RD. Chord consisting of 12 different notes, arranged in thirds, and forming 4 mutually exclusive triads.

COMPLEMENTARY SCALES. Melodic progressions of two octaves in range, comprising all 12 tones of the chromatic scale (Example, C major scale plus the pentatonic scale on black keys).

CONJUNCT POLYTETRACHORD. Progression of 12 tetrachords traversing all 12 keys, with the terminal tone of one tetrachord being the initial tone of the next (Examples, Phrygian Polytetrachord, No. 830; Minor Polytetrachord, No. 832; Major Polytetrachord, No. 833).

CROSSING INTERVALS. [Nos. 1243-1250]. Two overlapping 6-tone rows comprising all 12 different tones, each row forming a progression of major or minor seconds, thirds, fourths, fifths and sixths.

DIAPENTE. Interval of 3½ tones; a perfect fifth.

DIATESSARON. Interval of 2½ tones; a perfect fourth.

DISJUNCT POLYTETRACHORD. Progression of 12 tetrachords traversing all 12 keys, with adjacent tetrachords separated by one diatonic degree (Examples, Disjunct Phrygian Polytetrachord, No. 951; Disjunct Minor Polytetrachord, No. 956; Disjunct Major Polytetrachord, No. 958; Disjunct Lydian Polytetrachord, No. 959).

DITONE. Interval of 2 whole tones; a major third.

GRANDMOTHER CHORD. Chord, invented by Nicolas Slonimsky on February 13, 1938, containing all 12 different tones and different intervals symmetrically invertible in relation to the central interval, the tritone, which is the inversion of itself; the intervallic structure being a row of alter-

natingly odd and even intervals (counted in semitones), the odd-numbered series forming a diminishing arithmetical progression, and the even-numbered series an increasing progression.

HEPTATONIC ARPEGGIOS. [Nos. 1088-1141]. Melodic progressions by thirds derived from Heptatonic scales.

HEPTATONIC SCALES. [Nos. 1034-1087]. Diatonic progressions of 7 degrees, such as major and minor scales and church modes, and also scales containing 1 or 2 augmented seconds.

INFRA-INTER-ULTRAPOLATION. Pattern formed by the insertion of notes below, between, and above the principal tones of a progression (Example, Pattern No. 341).

INFRAPOLATION. Insertion of a note below the principal tones of a progression (Example, Pattern 231).

INTERPOLATION. Insertion of one or more notes between the principal tones of a progression (Example, Scale No. 21).

INTER-ULTRAPOLATION. Insertion of 2 notes, one between the principal tones of a given progression, the other above the principal tone (Example, Pattern No. 123).

MAJOR BITONAL CHORD. Chord of 2 major triads usually in keys whose tonics are at the interval of a tritone, as C major and F♯ major.

MAJOR POLYTETRACHORD. A series of major tetrachords, conjunct or disjunct, covering all 12 major keys (Examples, No. 833 and No. 958).

MASTER CHORDS. Dominant-seventh chords with the fifth omitted, tabulated chromatically in 12 different keys, to be used in harmonizing scales and melodic patterns, and indicated by figures, enclosed in circles, from 1 to 12.

MINOR BITONAL CHORD. Chord consisting of 2 minor chords, usually with tonics at the interval of a tritone, as C minor and F♯ minor.

MINOR POLYTETRACHORD. A series of minor tetrachords, conjunct or disjunct, covering all 12 minor keys (Examples, No. 832 and No. 956).

MIRROR INTERVAL PROGRESSIONS. Scales and patterns in which the descending figure is the melodic inversion of the ascending figure (Example, Scale No. 1 ascending is the mirror inversion of Scale No. 4 descending).

MOTHER CHORD. Chord, introduced by Fritz Klein in 1921, containing all 12 tones and 11 different intervals.

MUTUALLY EXCLUSIVE TRIADS. Four triads (major, minor, diminished or augmented) comprising all 12 different tones (Example, C major, F♯ major, D minor, and G♯ minor).

NON-SYMMETRIC INTERPOLATION. Free insertion of additional notes between the principal tones.

OCTAVE POSITION. In four-part harmony, a triad with the root both in the melody and in the bass.

PALINDROMIC CANONS. Canons that read the same backward or forward.

PANDIATONIC HARMONY. Part-writing in chords freely combined from the 7 tones of the diatonic scale.

PANDIATONIC PROGRESSIONS. Tonal rows composed of all 7 different tones of the diatonic scale.

PATTERN. Melodic figure in which the direction changes from ascending to descending, or vice versa, before arriving at the terminal point (All infrapolated and ultrapolated progressions are patterns).

PENTATONIC SCALES. [Nos. 1142-1190]. Scales of 5 notes.

PERMUTATION. Distribution of notes of a given melodic pattern in different orders of succession.

PHRYGIAN POLYTETRACHORD. Polytetrachord composed of 12 conjunct or disjunct Phrygian tetrachords (1 semitone plus 2 whole tones), (Examples, No. 830 and No. 951).

PLURAL SCALES. Progressions formed by disjunct scales, as C major, D♭ major, D major, and E♭ major.

POLYRHYTHMIC SCALES. Simultaneous progressions in different rhythms.

POLYTETRACHORD. Progression of 12 tetrachords passing through all 12 keys conjunctly (with the last tone of one tetrachord coinciding with the first tone of the next), or disjunctly (with the terminal tone of the first tetrachord separated by a diatonic degree from the initial tone of the next).

POLYTONAL POLYRHYTHMIC SCALES. Simultaneous progressions in different keys and in different rhythms.

POLYTONAL SCALES. Scales in different tonalities played simultaneously.

PROGRESSION. General term for any scale or melodic pattern.

PROMETHEUS SCALE. [No. 50]. The 6-tone scale (C, D, E, F♯, A, B♭) used by Scriabin in his symphonic poem *Prometheus*.

PYRAMID CHORD. Chord, introduced by Fritz Klein in 1921, composed of a series of diminishing intervals from an octave to a semitone.

QUADRITONE. Interval of 4 whole tones; a minor sixth.

QUADRITONAL ARPEGGIOS. [Nos. 1251-1291]. Melodic progressions formed by 4 mutually exclusive triads, as C major, D minor, F♯ major, and G♯ minor.

QUARTAL CHORD. 12-tone chord arranged in perfect fourths.

QUINQUETONE. Interval of 5 whole tones; a minor seventh.

QUINTAN POSITION. In four-part harmony, a triad with the root in the bass and the fifth in the melody.

SCALE. Progression of tones changing its direction only at terminal points (All interpolated progressions are scales).

SEMITONE PROGRESSION. Scale consisting of consecutive semitones; a chromatic scale.

SEPTITONE. Interval of 7 whole tones; a major ninth.

SESQUI. Prefix signifying the addition of a semitone to a given interval (Sesquitone = 1½ tones; Sesquiquadritone = 4½ tones).

SESQUIQUADRITONE. Interval of 4½ tones; a major sixth.

SESQUIQUINQUETONE. Interval of 5½ tones; a major seventh.

SESQUITONE. Interval of 1½ tones; a minor third.

SPIRAL PATTERNS. Melodic progressions converging toward a central tone.

SYMMETRIC INTERPOLATION. Insertion of notes at equal intervals from respective pivotal points, resulting in invertible progressions (Example, Scale No. 37: C, D, F, F♯, G, B♭, C, in which the intervals are the same from C upward and from the upper C downward).

TERTIAN POSITION. In four-part harmony, a triad with the root in the bass and the third in the melody.

TONE-CLUSTER. Term, introduced by Henry Cowell, signifying a complex of notes filling one or more octaves, diatonically, chromatically, or pentatonically.

TRITONE. Interval of 3 whole tones; an augmented fourth, or a diminished fifth.

TWELVE-TONE PROGRESSIONS. Melodic figures of 12 different tones.

ULTRAPOLATION. Insertion of one or more notes above a principal tone of a scale (Example, Pattern No. 53, in which G is inserted above F♯).

WHOLE-TONE CHORDS. Chords composed of intervals of one or several whole tones each.

Tritone Progression

Equal Division of One Octave into Two Parts

Interpolation of One Note

①②③④⑤⑥⑦⑧⑨⑩⑪⑫ indicate Master Chords.

Interpolation of Two Notes

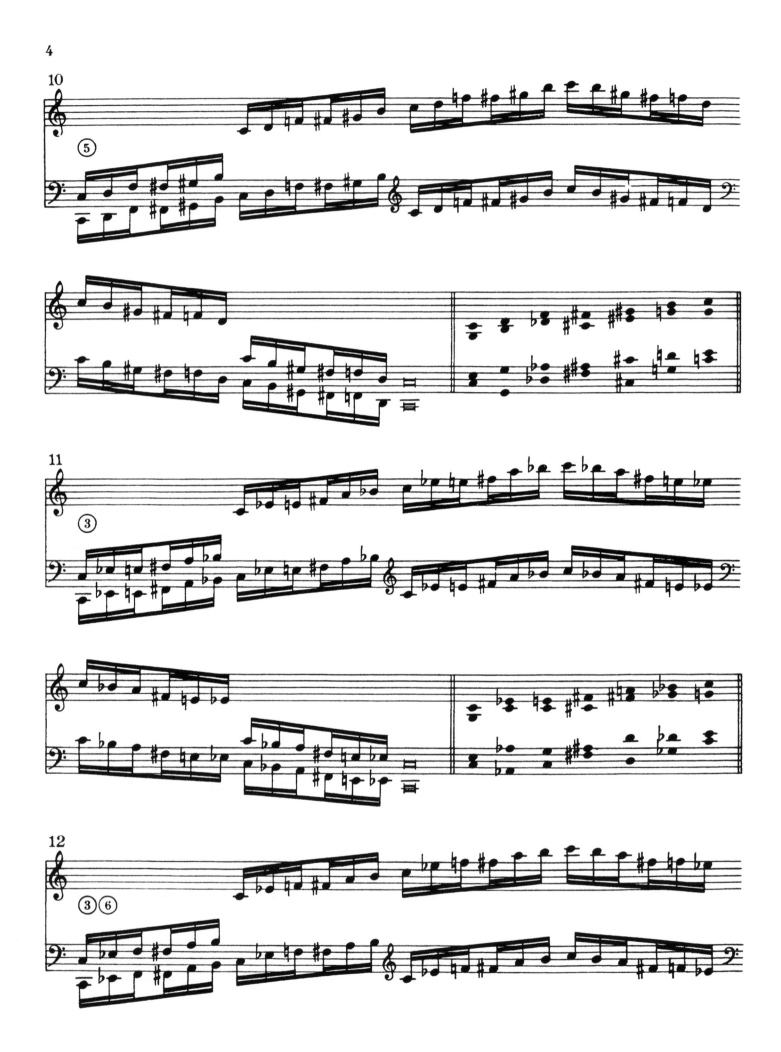

Interpolation of Three Notes

Interpolation of Four Notes

Symmetric Interpolation of One Note

Symmetric Interpolation of Two Notes

13

Symmetric Interpolation of Three Notes

Non-Symmetric Interpolation

Ultrapolation of One Note

Ultrapolation of Two Notes

16

Ultrapolation of Three Notes

Infrapolation of One Note

Infrapolation of Two Notes

18

Infrapolation of Three Notes

Infra-Interpolation

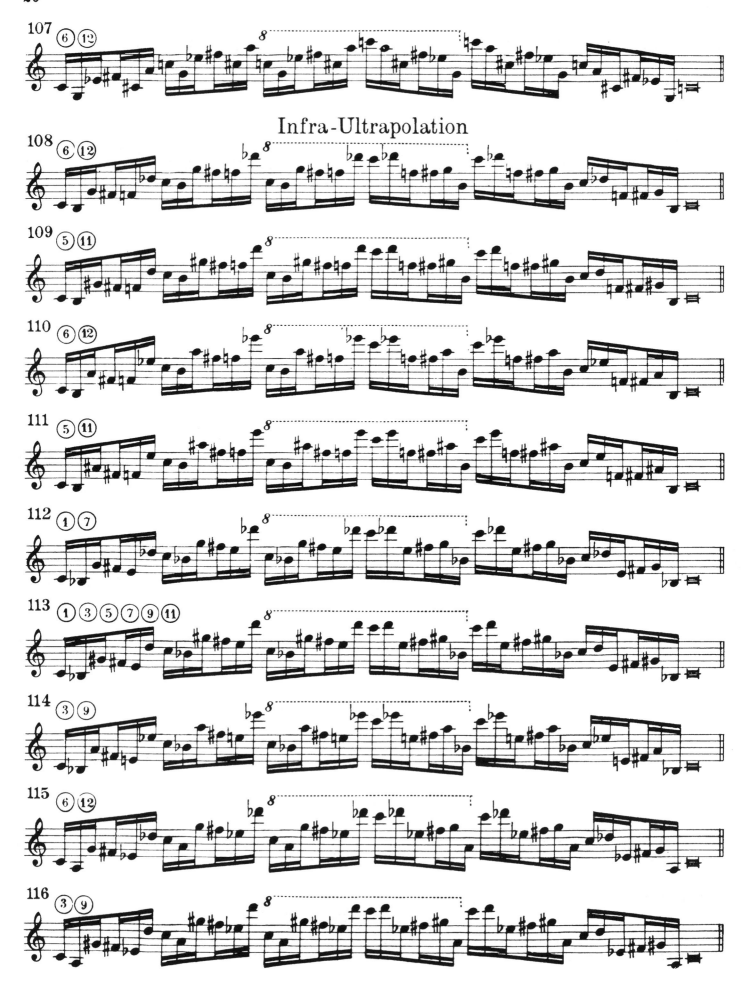

Infra-Ultrapolation

Inter-Ultrapolation

22

Infra-Inter-Ultrapolation

Ditone Progression
Equal Division of One Octave into Three Parts

Interpolation of One Note

Interpolation of Two Notes

184 [Scale of A. Tcherepnin]

185

Ultrapolation of One Note

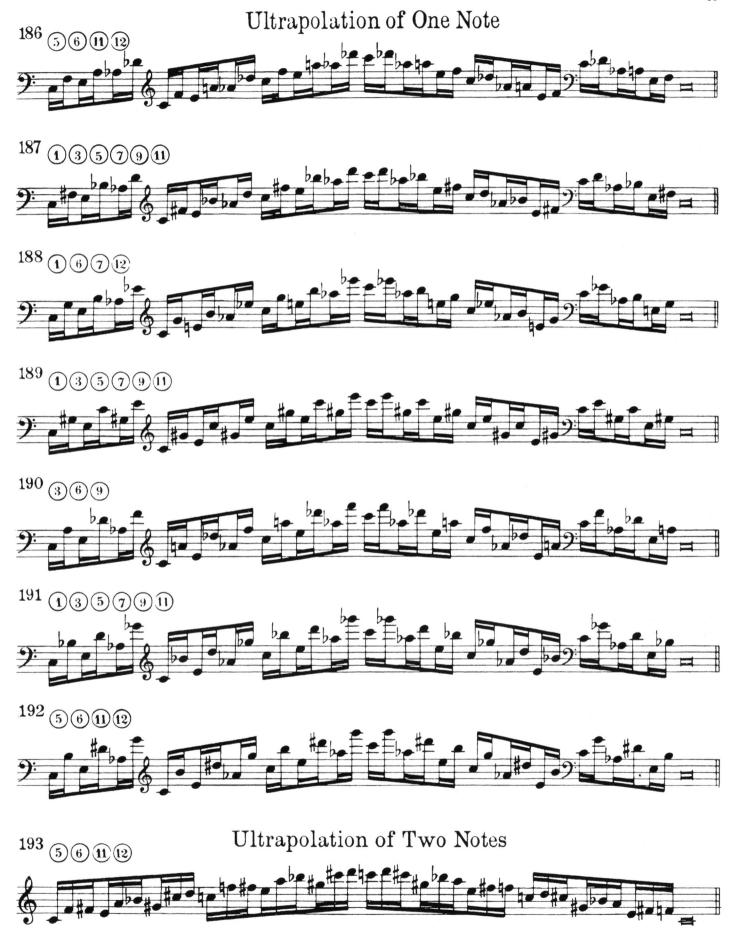

Ultrapolation of Two Notes

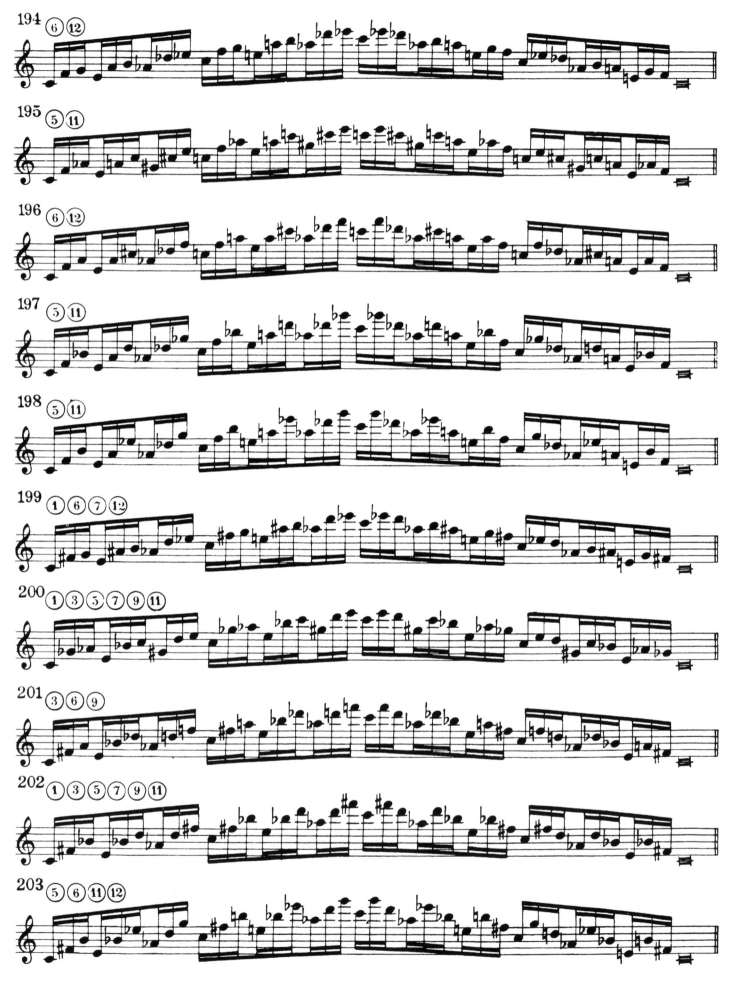

Ultrapolation of Three Notes

34

Infrapolation of One Note

Infrapolation of Two Notes

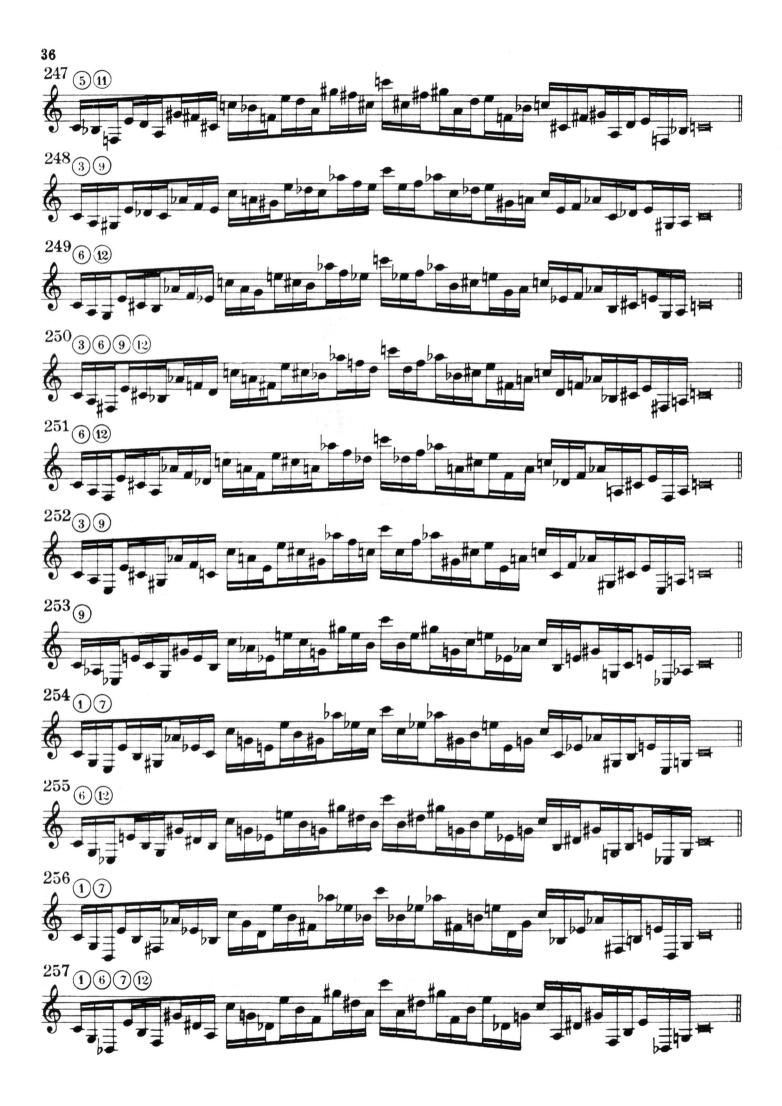

Infrapolation of Three Notes

Infra-Interpolation

Infra-Ultrapolation

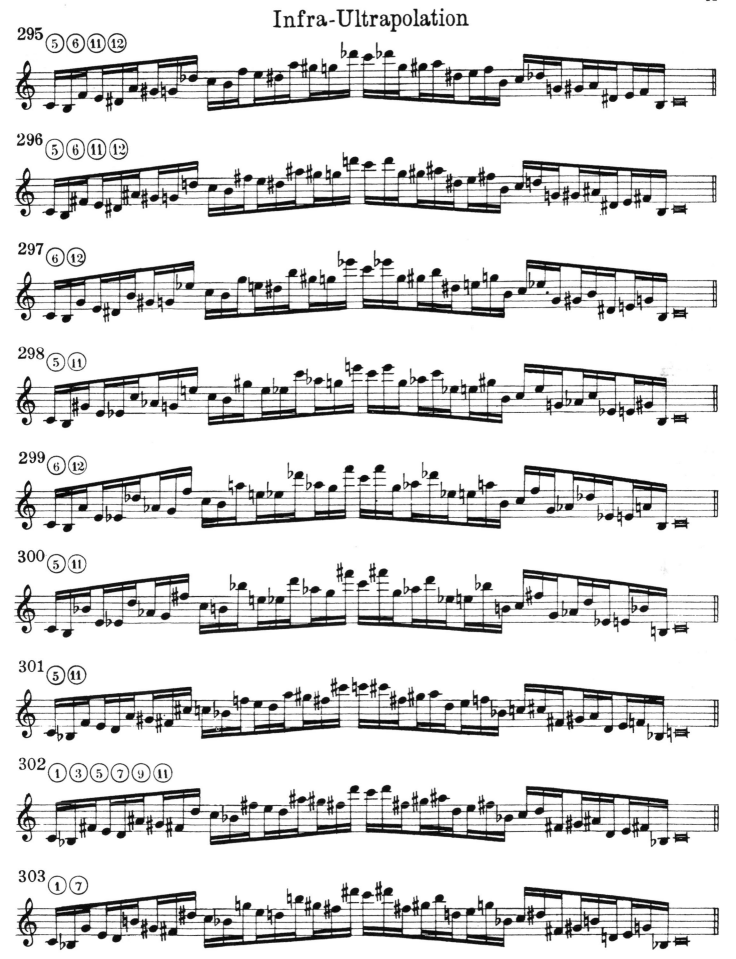

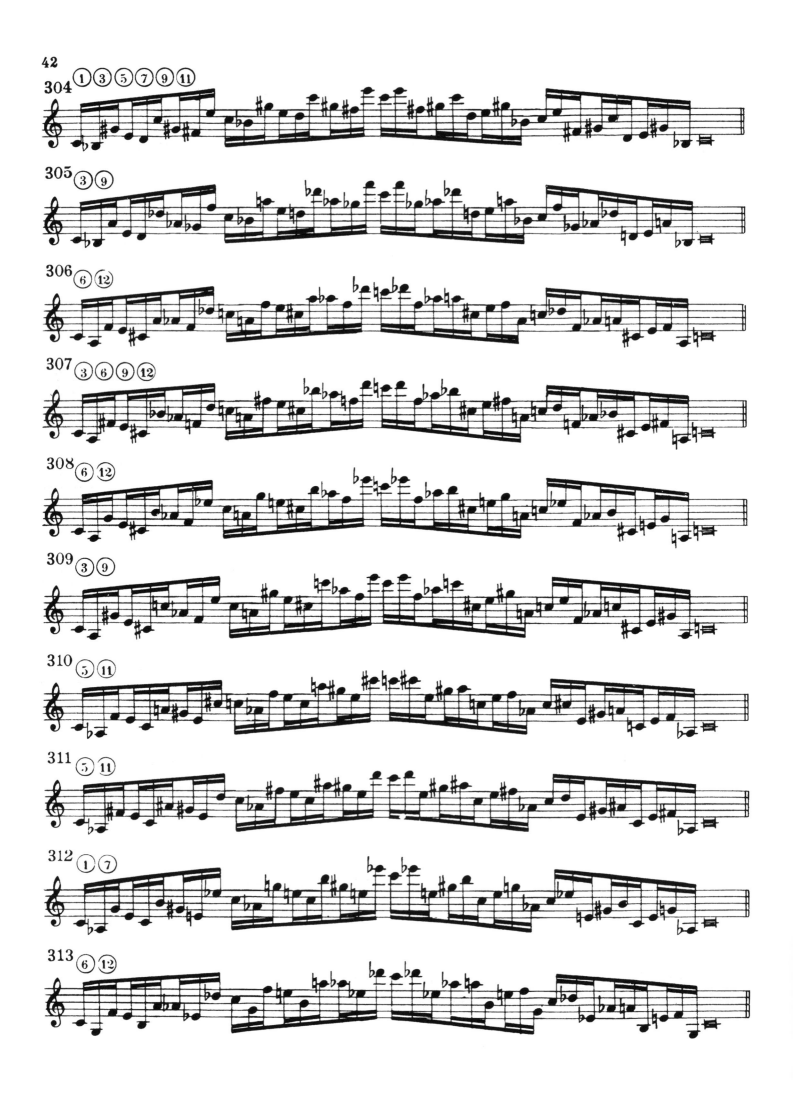

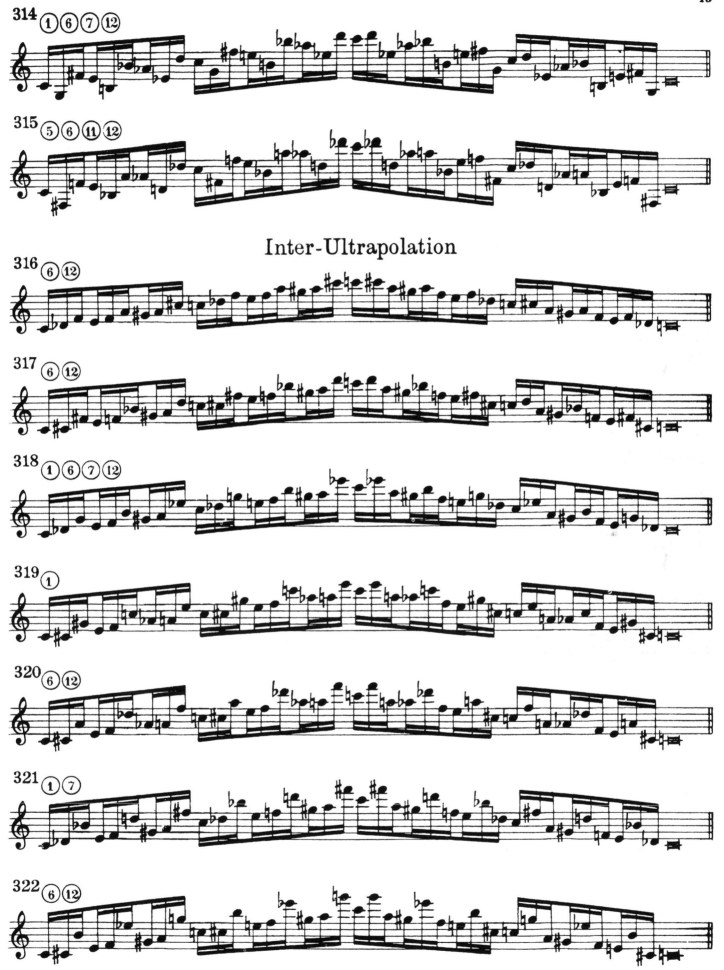

Inter-Ultrapolation

Infra-Inter-Ultrapolation

Miscellaneous Patterns

Sesquitone Progression

Equal Division of One Octave into Four Parts

Interpolation of One Note

Ultrapolation of One Note

Ultrapolation of Two Notes

Ultrapolation of Three Notes

Infrapolation of One Note

Infrapolation of Two Notes

Infrapolation of Three Notes

[Rimsky-Korsakov: Battle Scene from the Opera *Kitezh*]

Infra - Interpolation

64

Inter-Ultrapolation

Infra-Ultrapolation

Infra-Inter-Ultrapolation

Miscellaneous Patterns

Whole-Tone Progression

Equal Division of One Octave into Six Parts

Harmonizations

Ultrapolation of One Note

Infrapolation of One Note

Infra-Interpolation

Infra-Ultrapolation

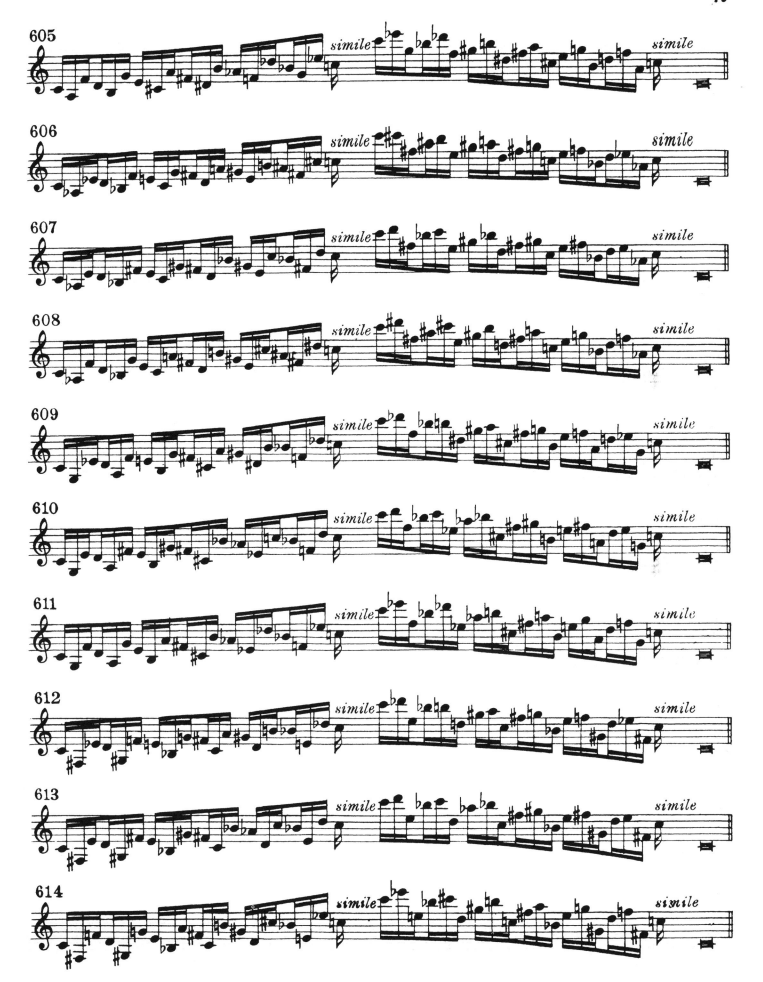

Inter-Ultrapolation

Infra-Inter-Ultrapolation

Semitone Progression

Equal Division of One Octave into Twelve Parts

Harmonization

88

645

Harmonization

646

647

Harmonization

or

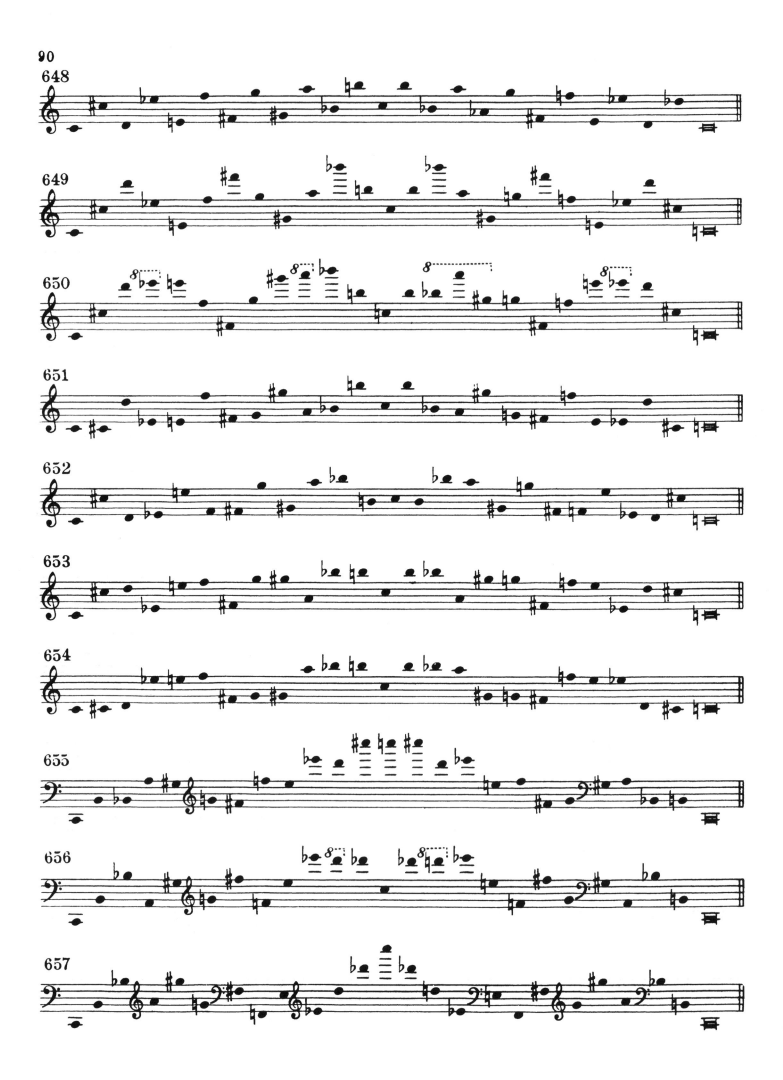

Quadritone Progression

Equal Division of Two Octaves into Three Parts

Interpolation of One Note

663

Interpolation of Two Notes

664

665

666

667

668

669

670

671

672

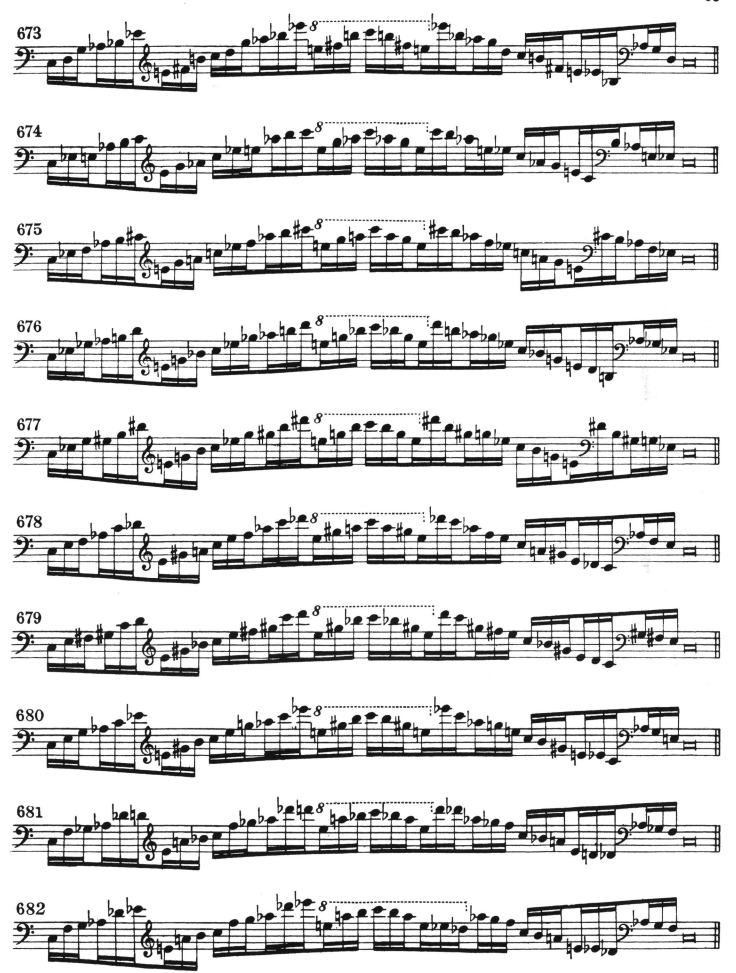

Interpolation of Three Notes

Interpolation of Four Notes

Ultrapolation of One Note

98

Infrapolation of One Note

[Rimsky-Korsakov: *Coq d'or*, Scene II]

Inter-Infrapolation

Ultra-Interpolation

729

730

731

732

Inter-Infra-Ultrapolation

733

734 [12 tones]

735 [12 tones]

736 [12 tones]

Sesquiquadritone Progression
Equal Division of Three Octaves into Four Parts

Interpolation of One Note

Interpolation of Two Notes

Interpolation of Three Notes

Interpolation of Four Notes

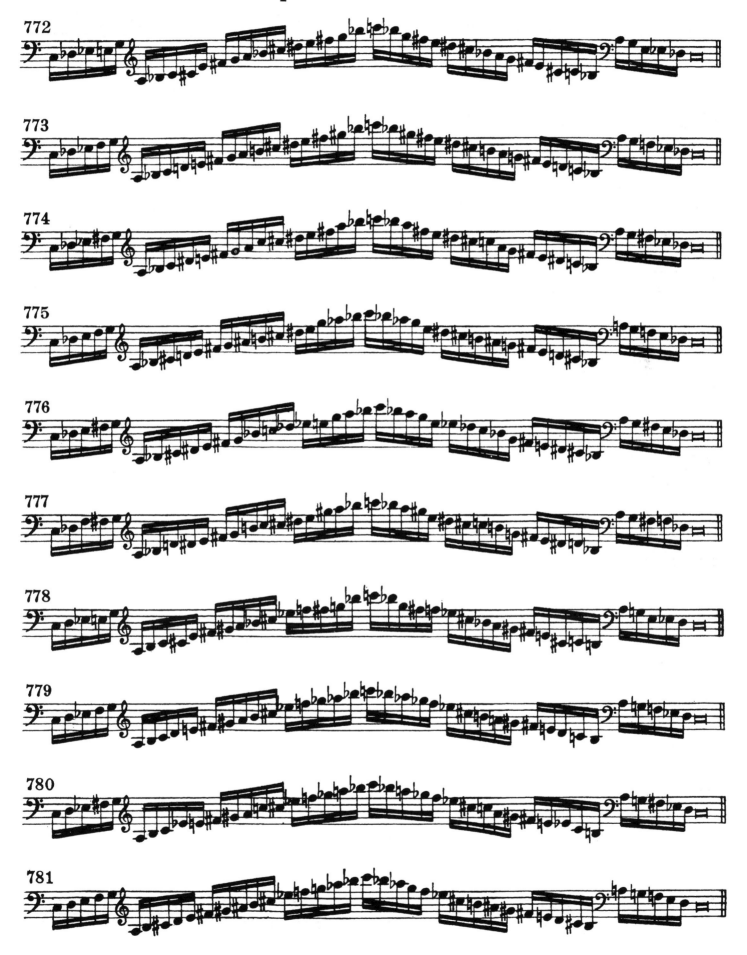

782

783

Ultrapolation of One Note

784 785

786 787

788

Infrapolation of One Note

789 790

791 792

Infra-Ultrapolation

793

794

795

Inter-Infrapolation

Inter-Infra-Interpolation

Ultra-Infra-Interpolation

Inter-Ultrapolation

Quinquetone Progression
Equal Division of Five Octaves into Six Parts

Interpolation of Two Notes

Interpolation of Three Notes

Ultrapolation of One Note

Infrapolation of One Note

Diatessaron Progression
Equal Division of Five Octaves into Twelve Parts

Interpolation of One Note

Interpolation of Two Notes

831

832 Minor Polytetrachord

Major Polytetrachord

833

834

835

836

837

Ultrapolation of One Note

838

839

Ultrapolation of Two Notes

Ultrapolation of Three Notes

Infrapolation of One Note

Infrapolation of Two Notes

Infrapolation of Three Notes

Infra - Interpolation.

912

Miscellaneous Patterns

913

914

915

916

917

918

919

920

Septitone Progression
Equal Division of Seven Octaves into Six Parts

Interpolation of Two Notes

Interpolation of Three Notes

[Béla Bartók: Mikrokosmos, №143]

Diapente Progression

Equal Division of Seven Octaves into Twelve Parts

Interpolation of One Note

Interpolation of Two Notes

Interpolation of Three Notes

948

949

950

Disjunct Phrygian Polytetrachord

951

952

953

954

955

Disjunct Minor Polytetrachord

956

957

958 Disjunct Major Polytetrachord

959 Disjunct Lydian Polytetrachord

960

961

962

963

964

Ultrapolation of One Note

965

966

967

Ultrapolation of Two Notes

Infrapolation of One Note

131

Infrapolation of Two Notes

Infra-Interpolation

Infra-Ultrapolation

Inter-Ultrapolation

134

Infra-Inter-Ultrapolation

Sesquiquinquetone Progression
Equal Division of Eleven Octaves into Twelve Parts

Interpolation of One Note

Interpolation of Two Notes

Heptatonic Scales

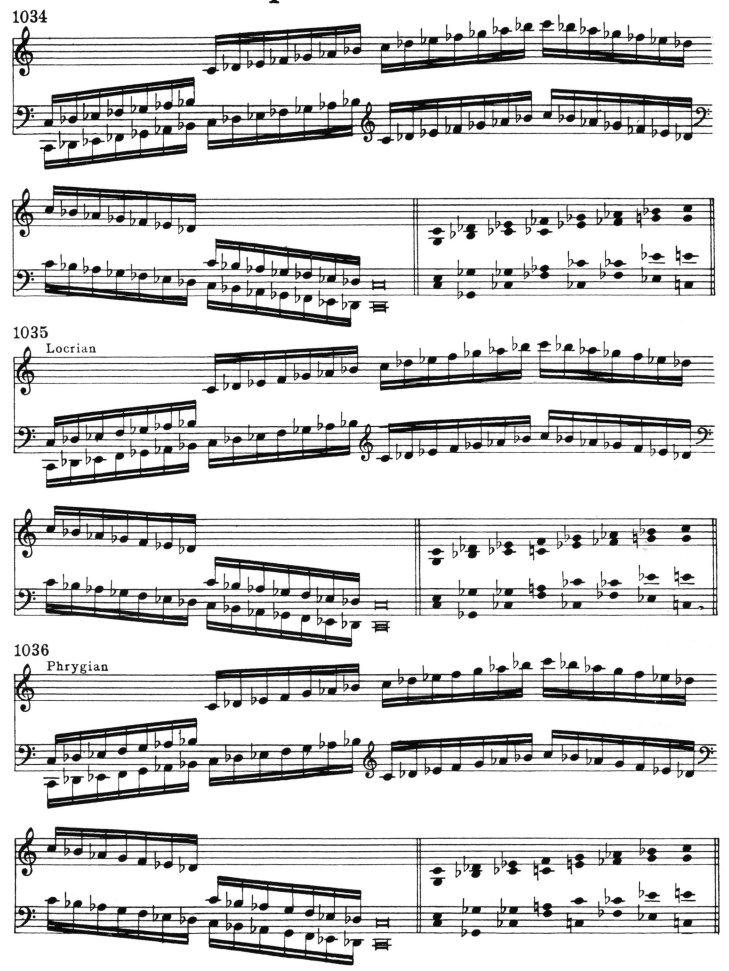

138

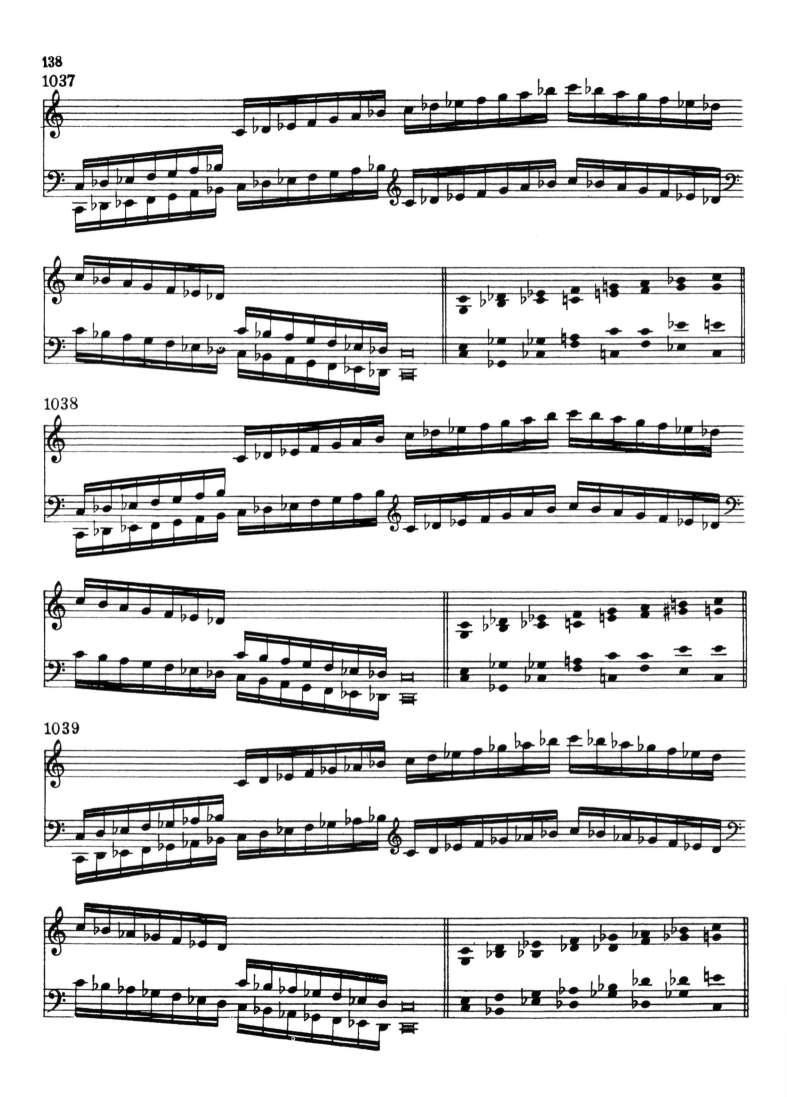

140

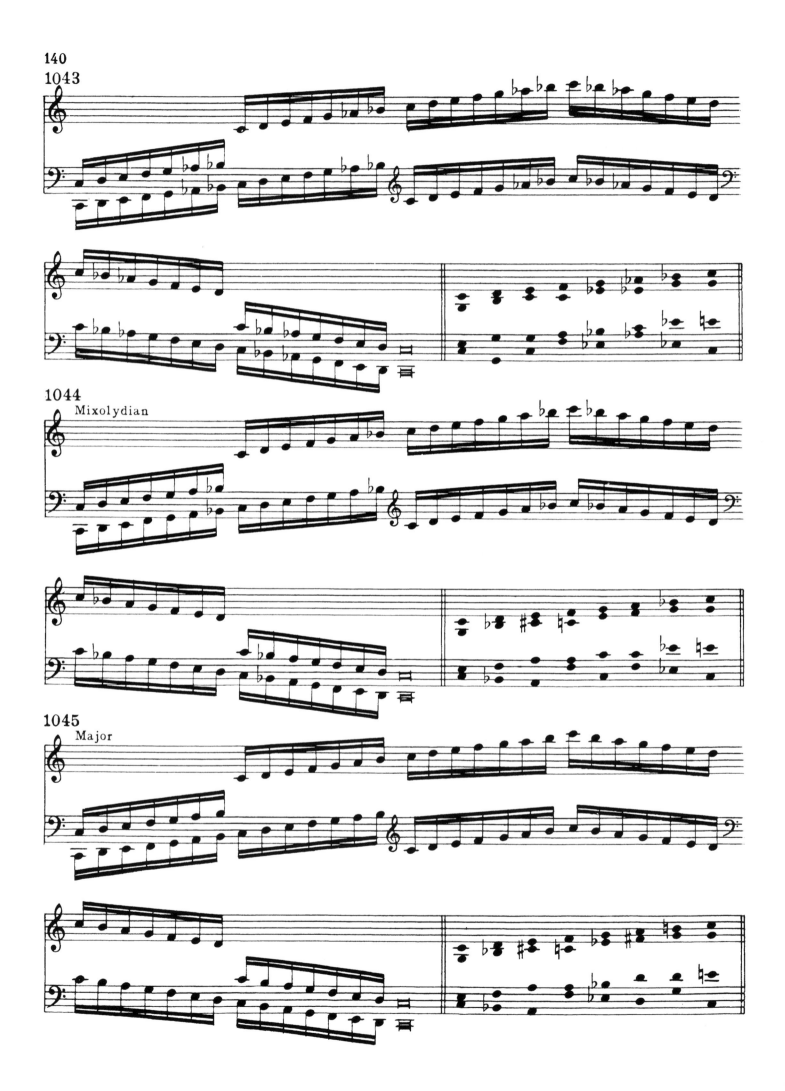

1046 [Howard Hanson: Symphony № 4]

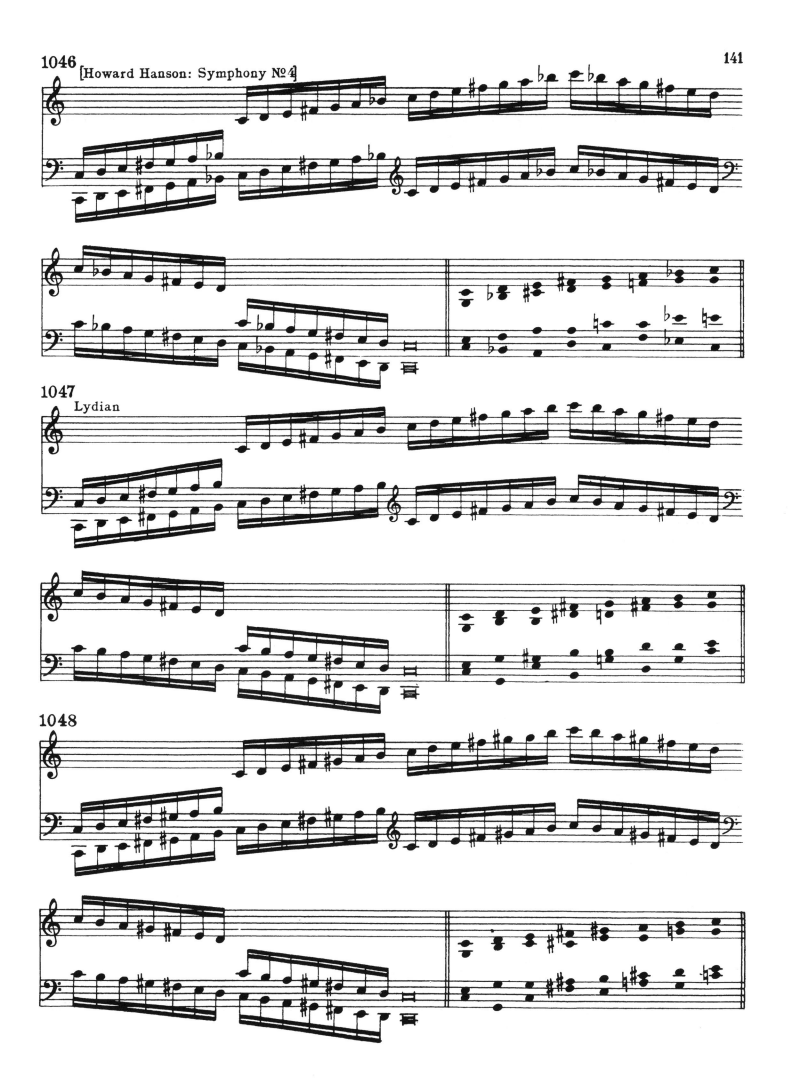

1047
Lydian

1048

Heptatonic Scales with an Augmented Second

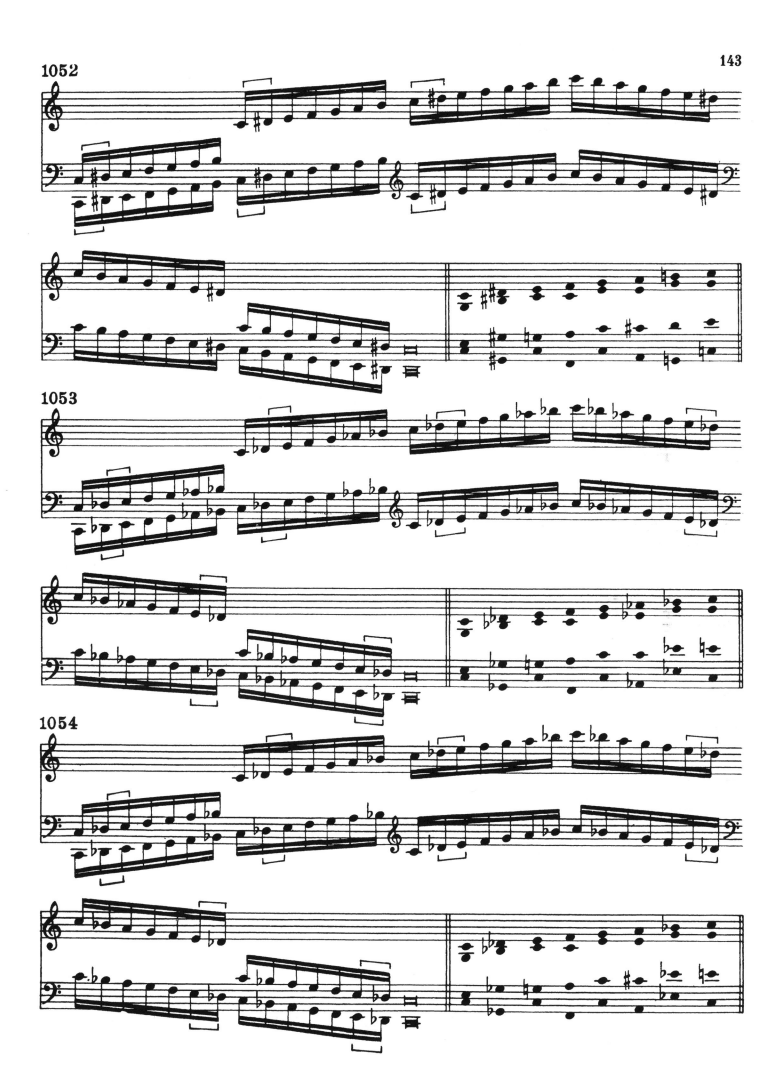

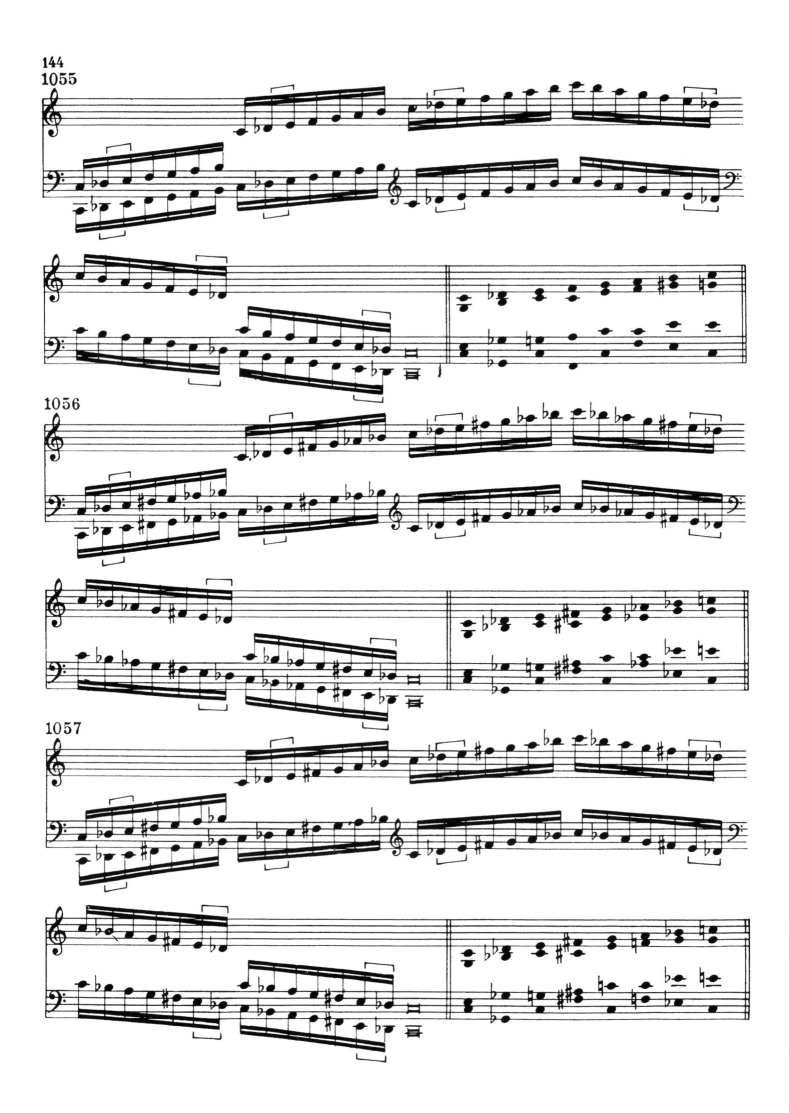

1058

1059

"Enigmatic Scale" of Verdi

1060

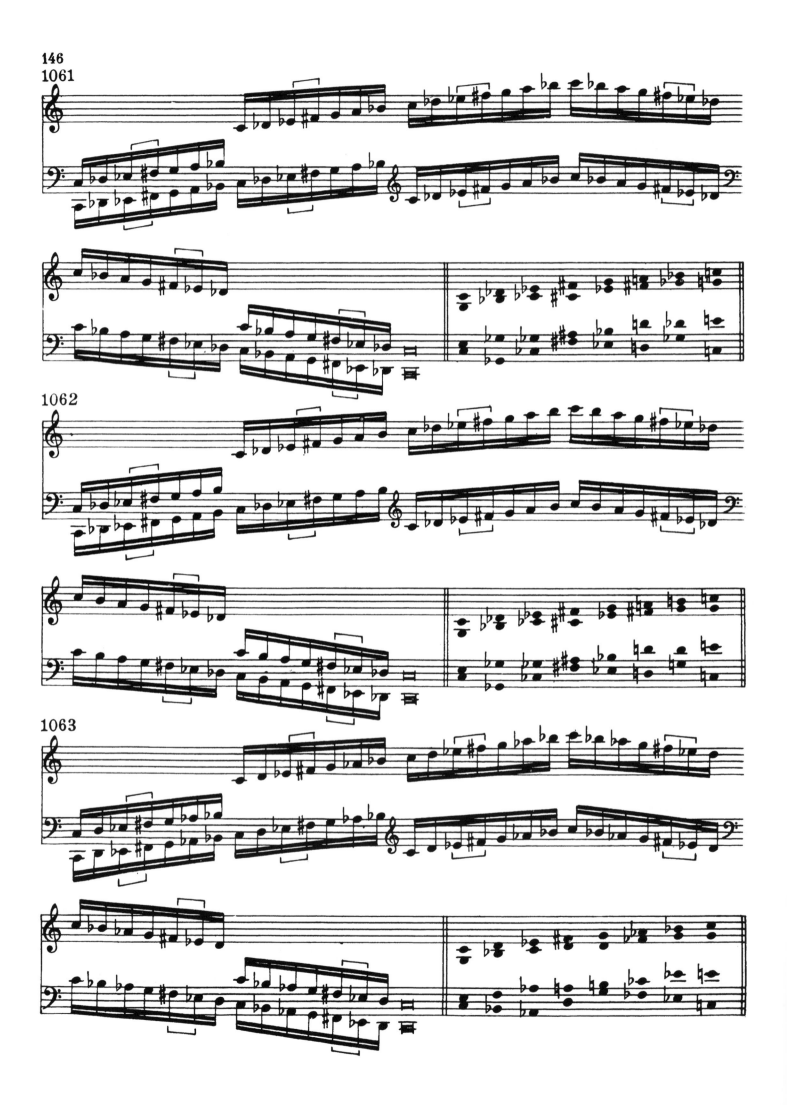

1064

1065

1066

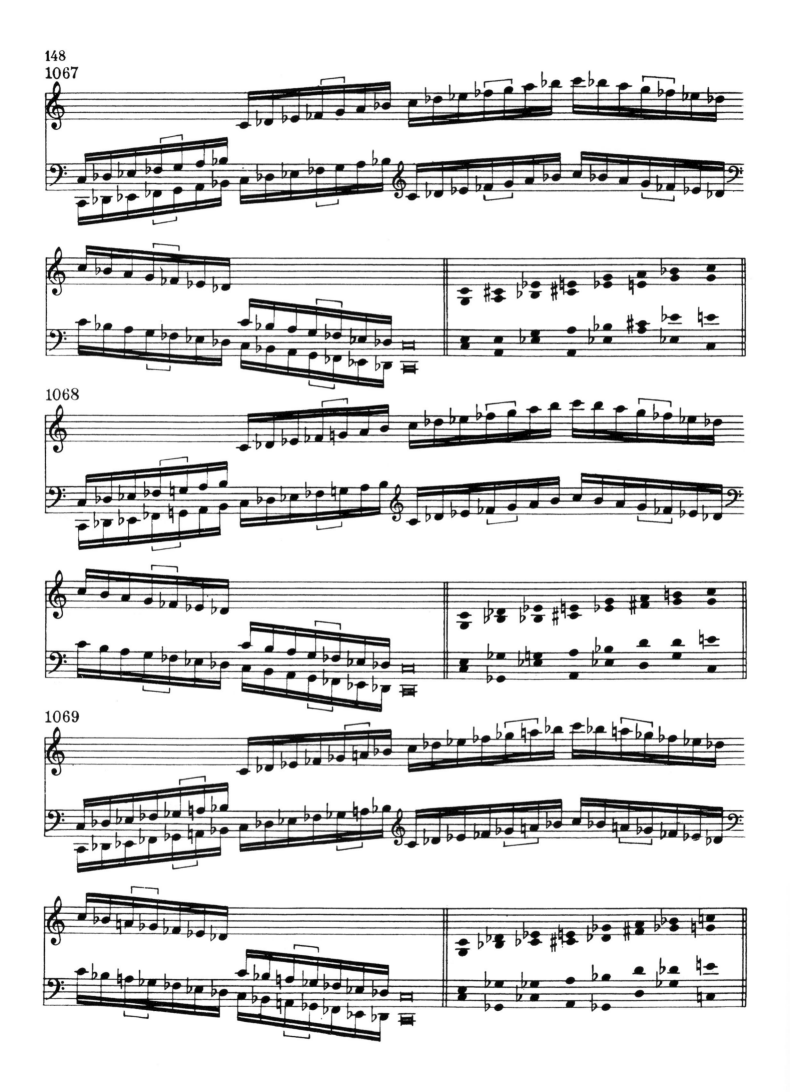

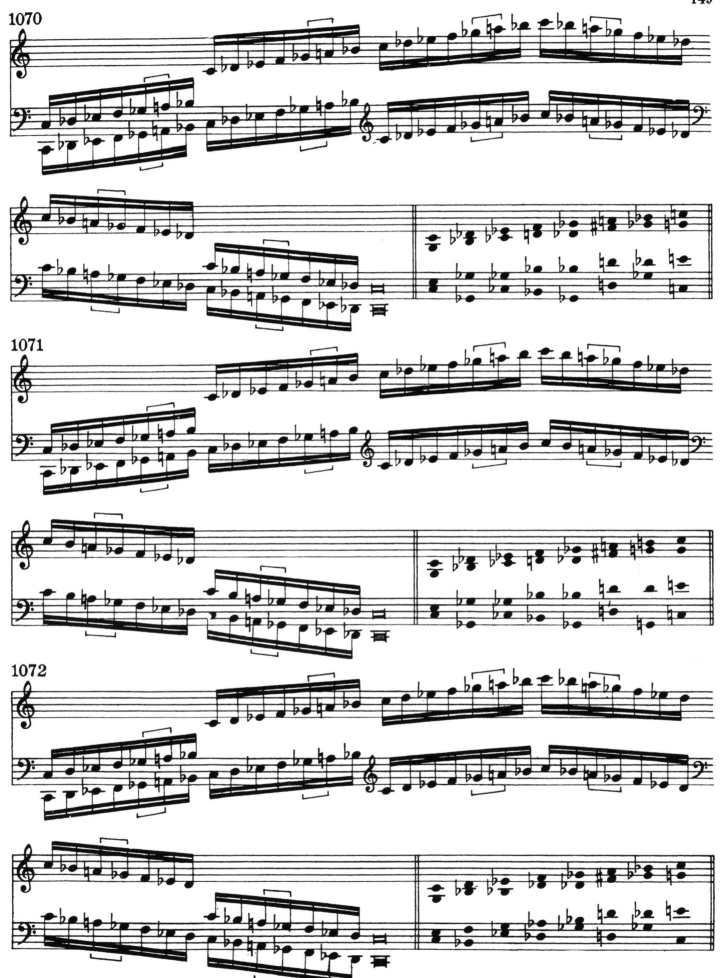

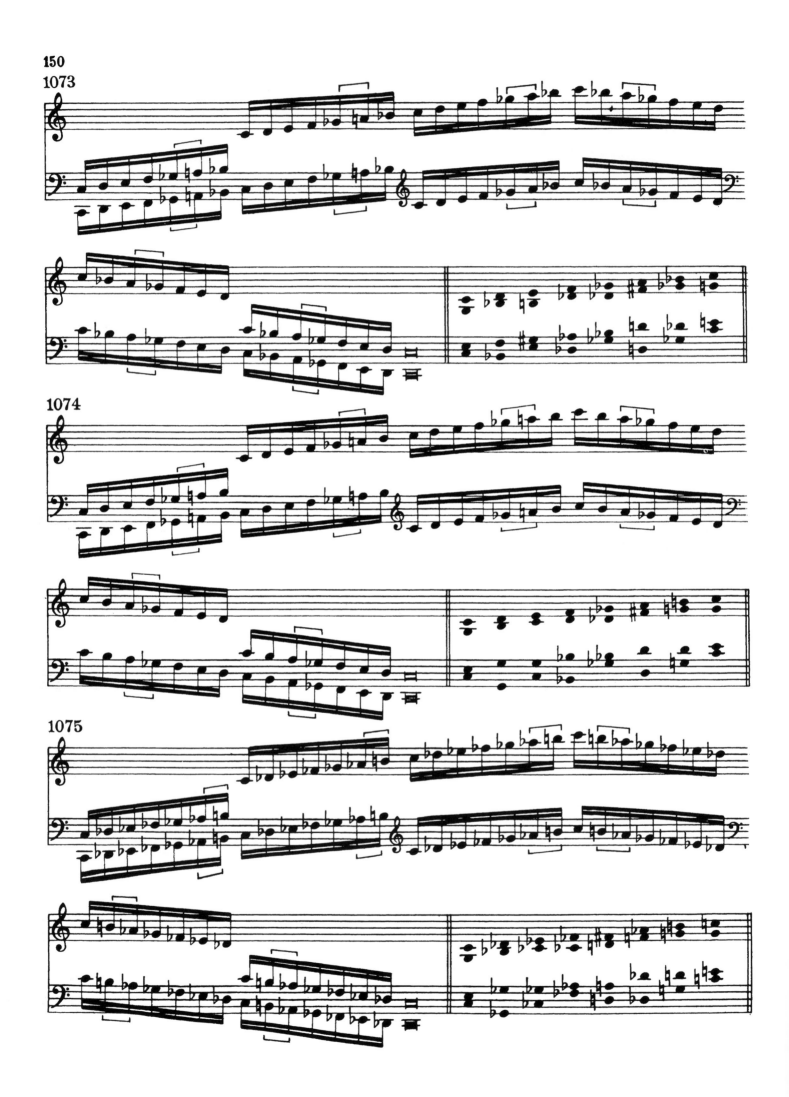

1076

1077

1078
Minor Harmonic

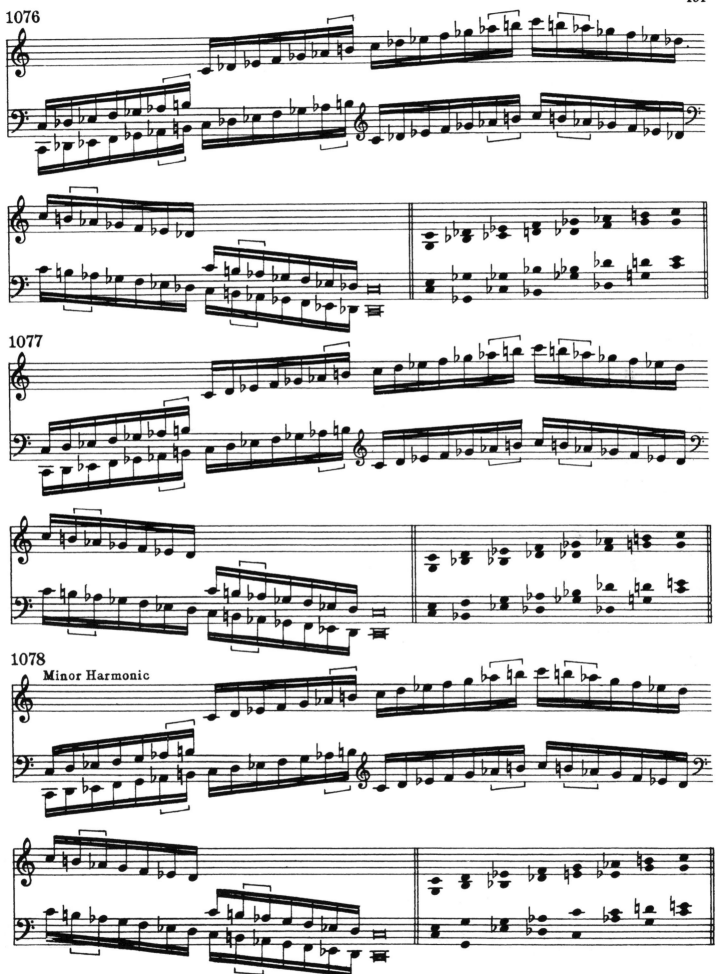

1079 Major Harmonic

Heptatonic Scales with Two Augmented Seconds

1080

1081

1082

1083

1084

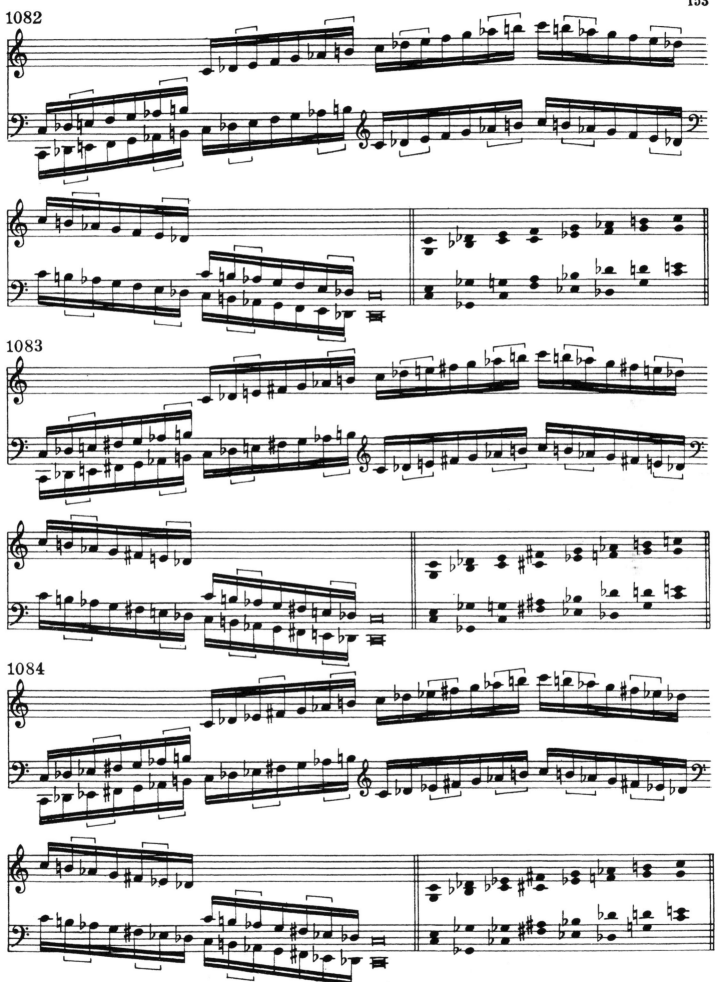

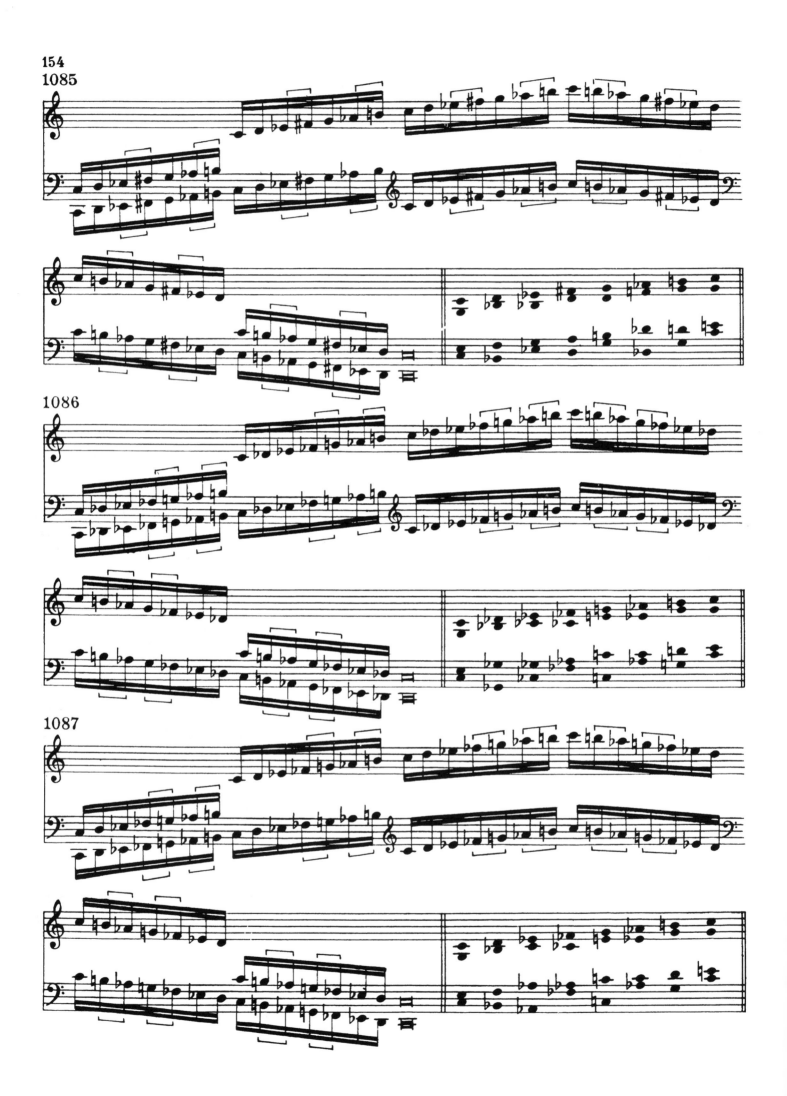

Heptatonic Arpeggios

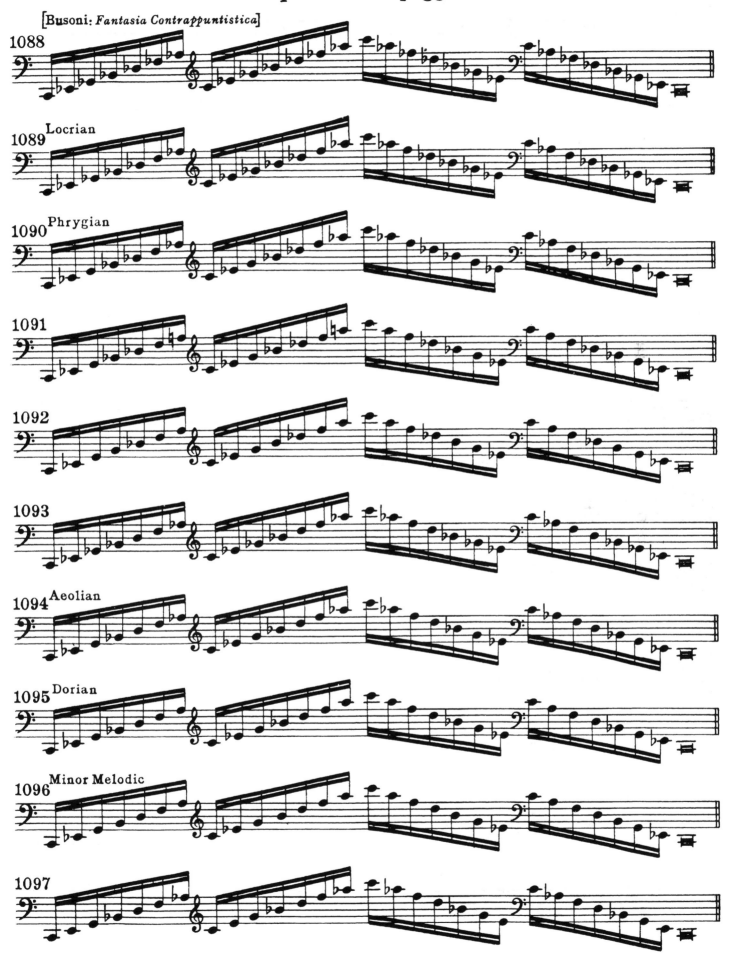

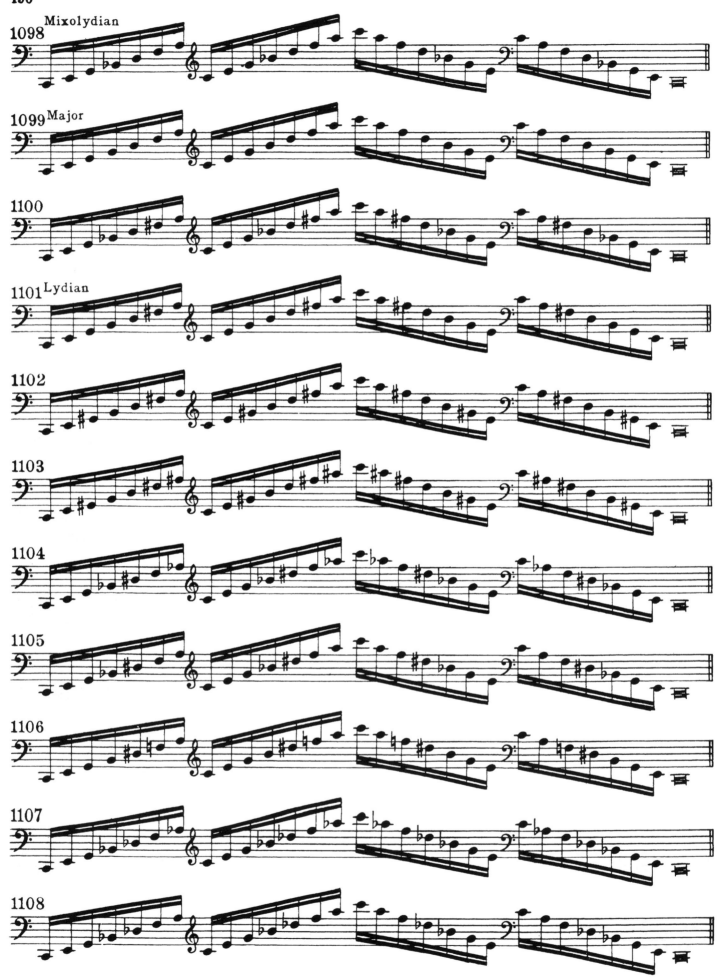

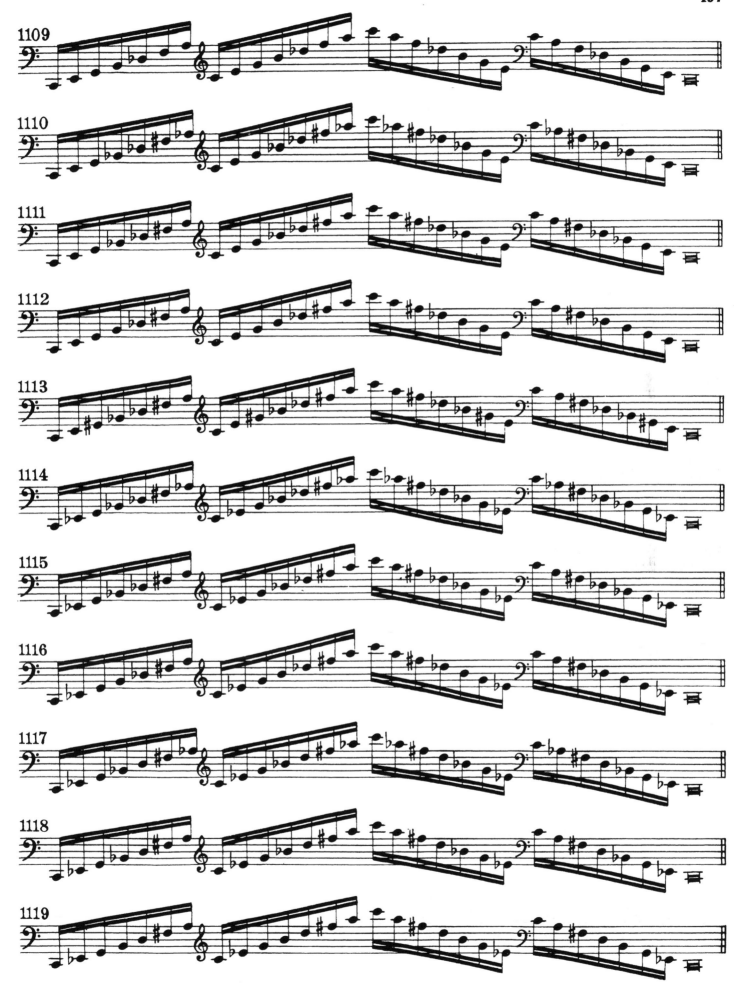

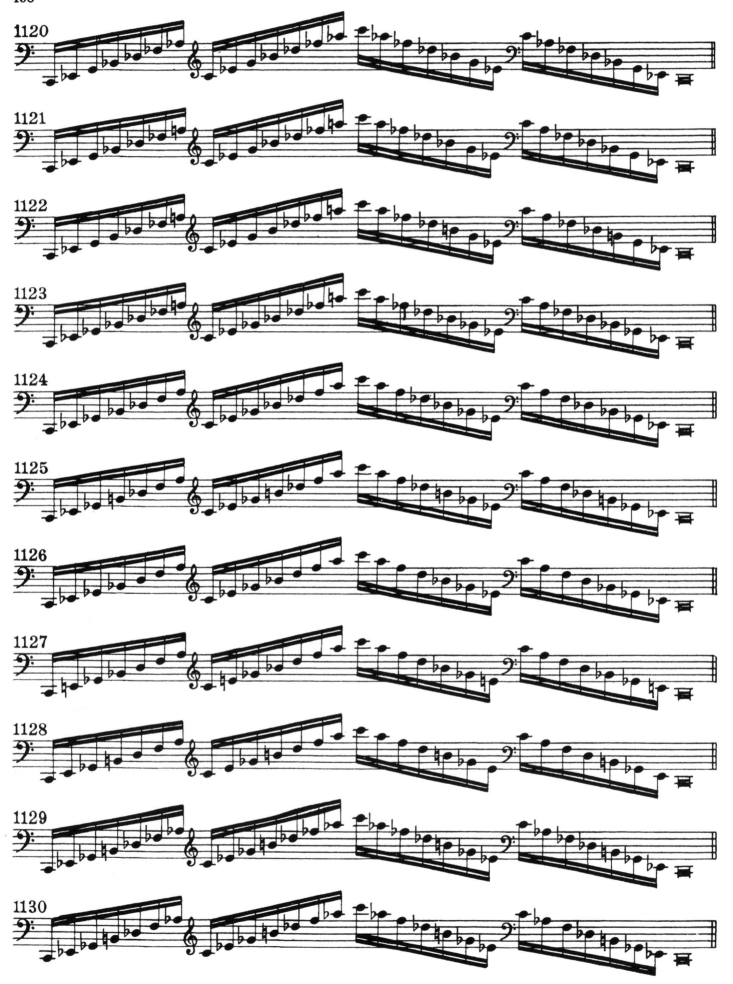

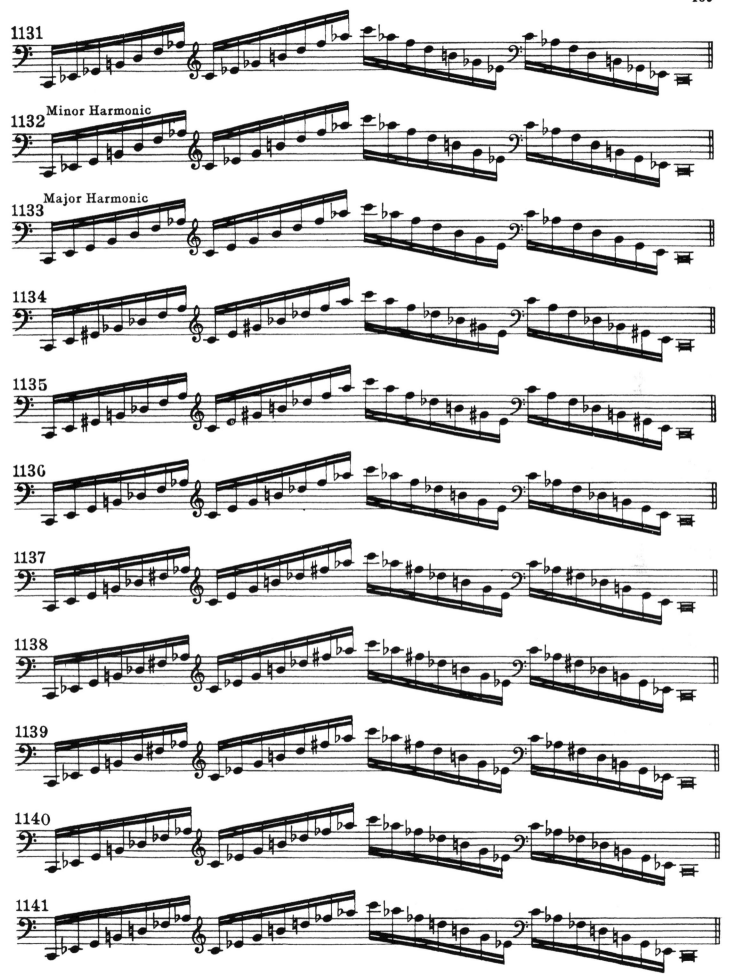

Pentatonic Scales

1142

1143

1144 Javanese *Pelog* Scale

1145

1146

162

1152

1153 Japanese *Hira-Joshi* Scale

1154

1155

1156

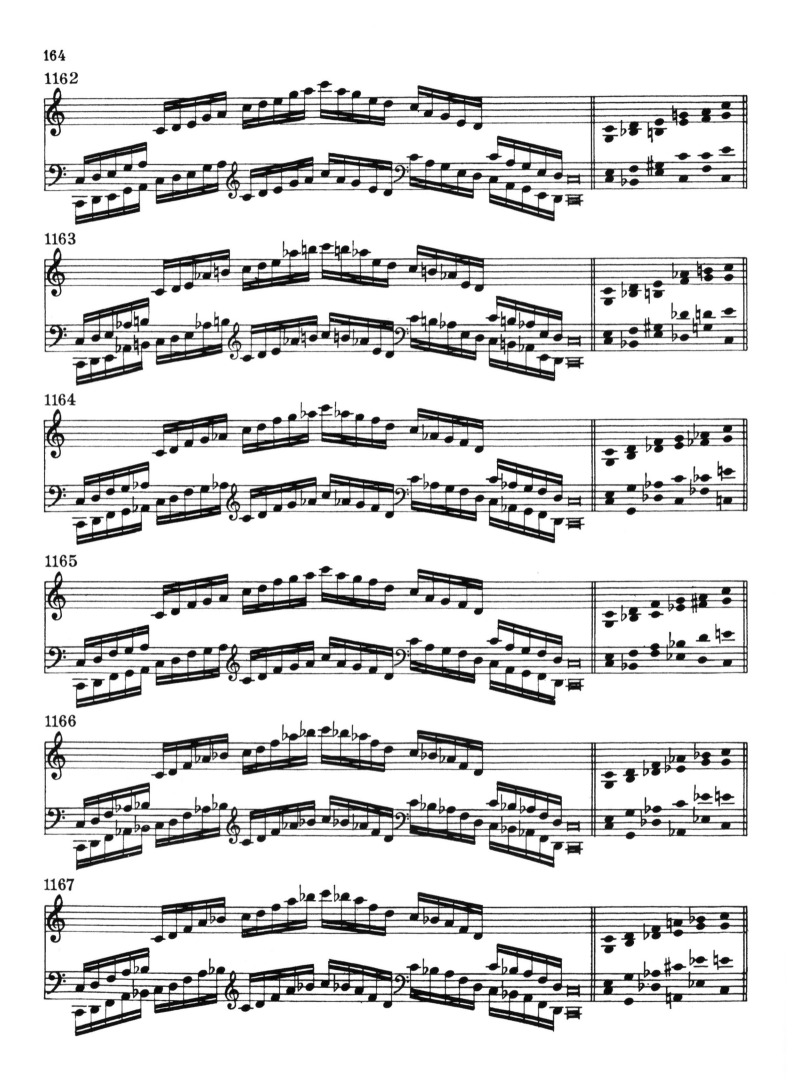

Bitonal Arpeggios

1191 C Major & C Minor

1192 C Major & Db Major

1193 C Major & C# Minor

1194 C Major & D Major

1195 C Major & D Minor

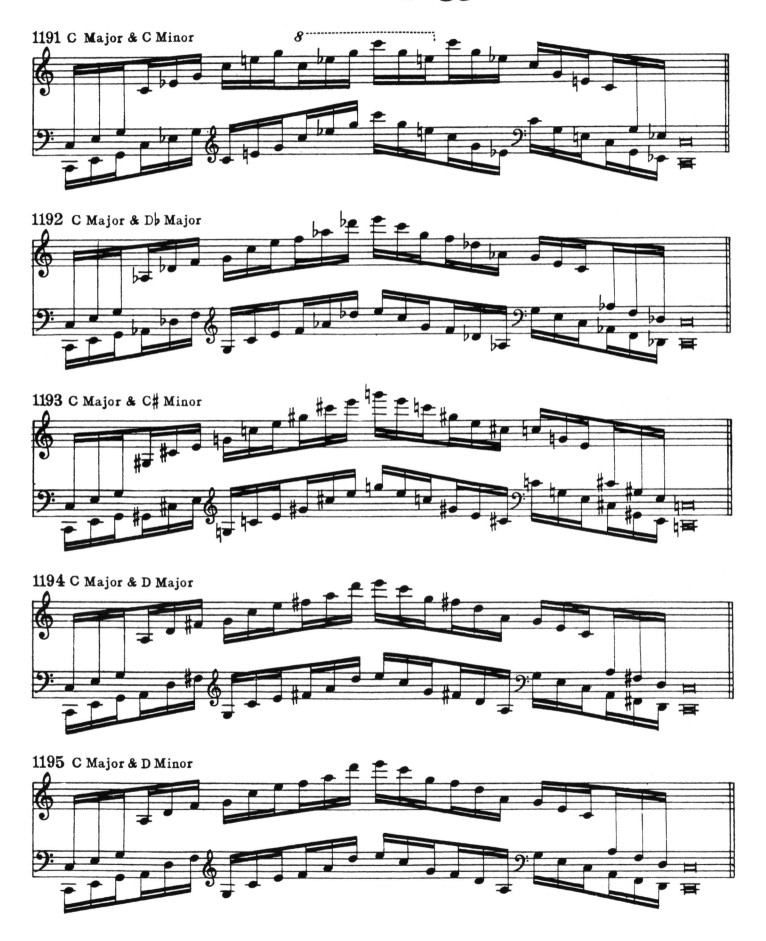

1202 C Major & F# Major

1203 C Major & F# Minor

1204 C Major & G Major

1205 C Major & G Minor

1206 C Major & Ab Major

1207 C Major & G# Minor

1208 C Major & A Major

1209 C Major & A Minor

1210 C Major & Bb Major

1211 C Major & Bb Minor

1212 C Major & B Major

1213 C Major & B Minor

Twelve-Tone Patterns
Dodecaphonic

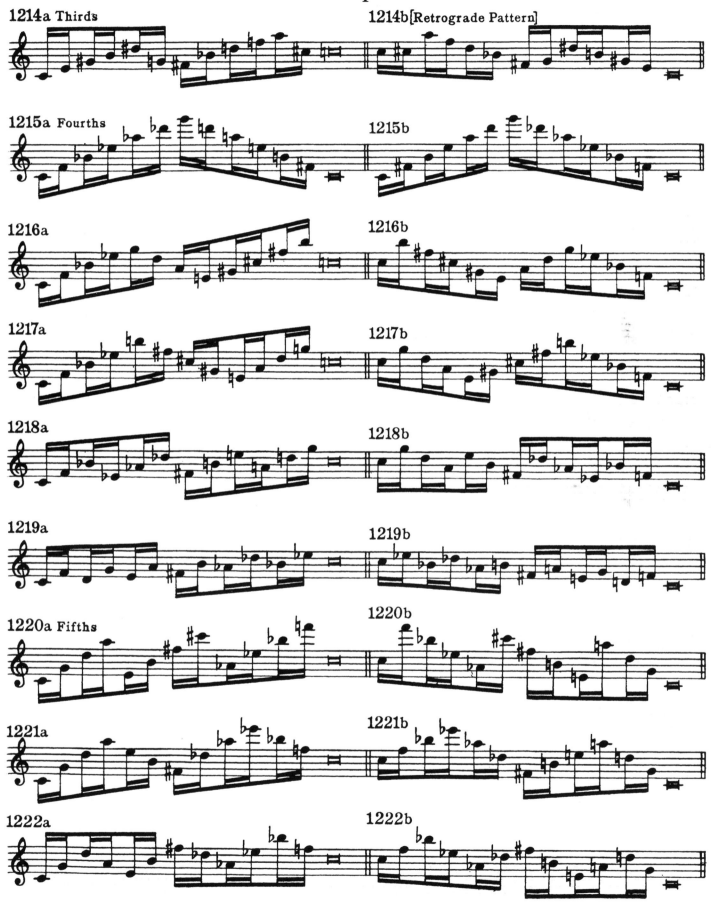

Twelve-Tone Spirals

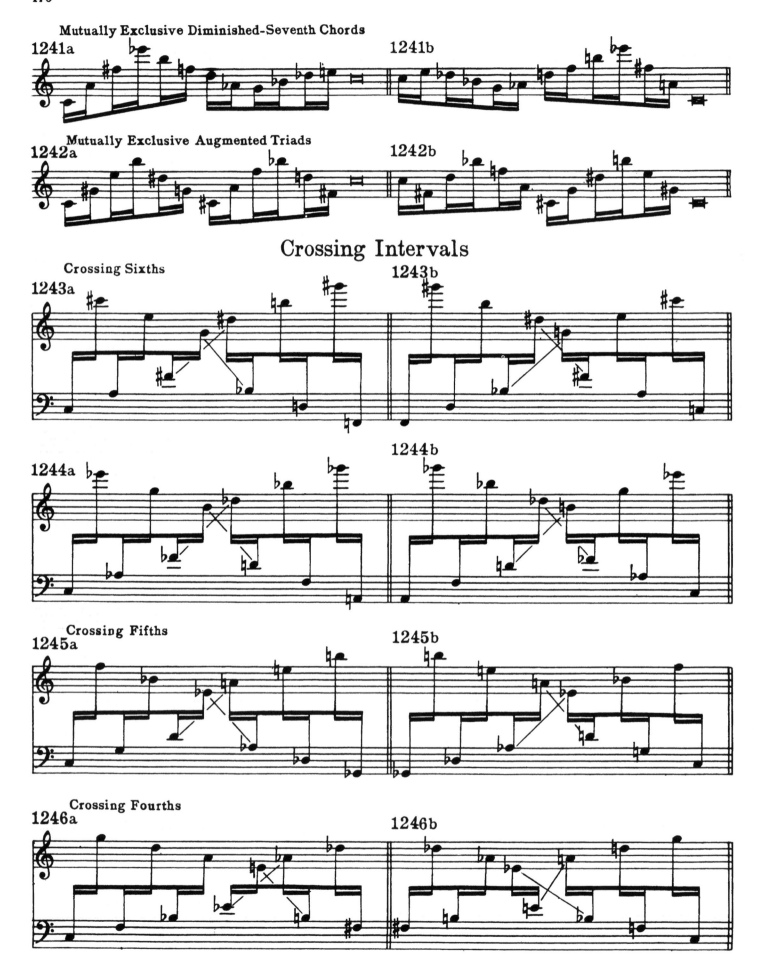

1247a Crossing Thirds **1247b**

Division of Twelve Tones into Four Mutually Exclusive Triads

Two Major and Two Minor Triads

Two Augmented, One Major, One Minor Triads

Augmented, Major, Minor, Diminished Triads

Two Diminished, One Major, One Minor Triads

Four Augmented Triads

Quadritonal Arpeggios

1251

1252

1253

1254

1255 [Slonimsky: *Moto Perpetuo*]

1256

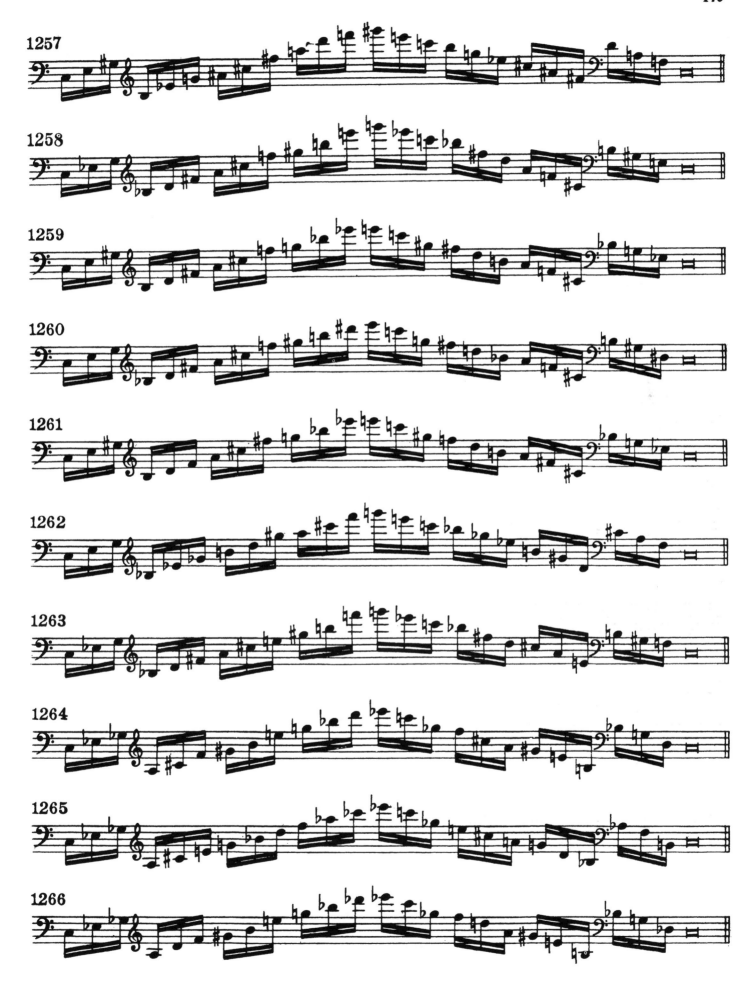

Miscellaneous Dodecaphonic Patterns

1293 Two Major Hexachords

Invertible Dodecaphonic Progressions
With All Different Intervals

(Figures indicate number of semitones)

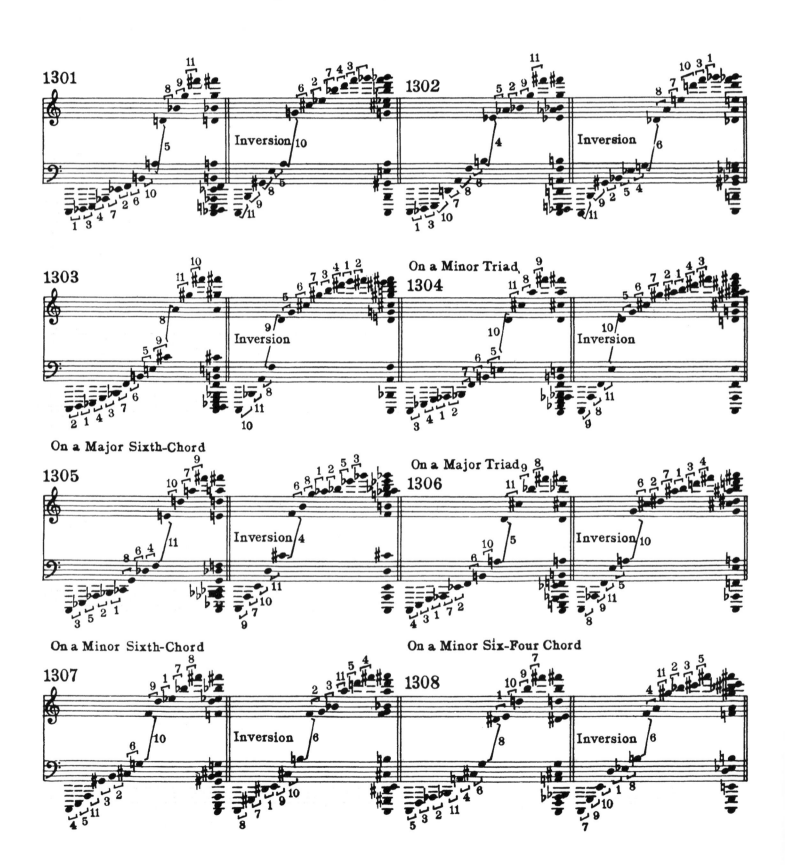

On a Major Six-Four Chord

White-Key Row of Six Notes

White-Key Row of Six Notes

White-Key Row of Six Notes

Mother Chord

Grandmother Chord

Intervallic Series

Increasing and Diminishing Intervals

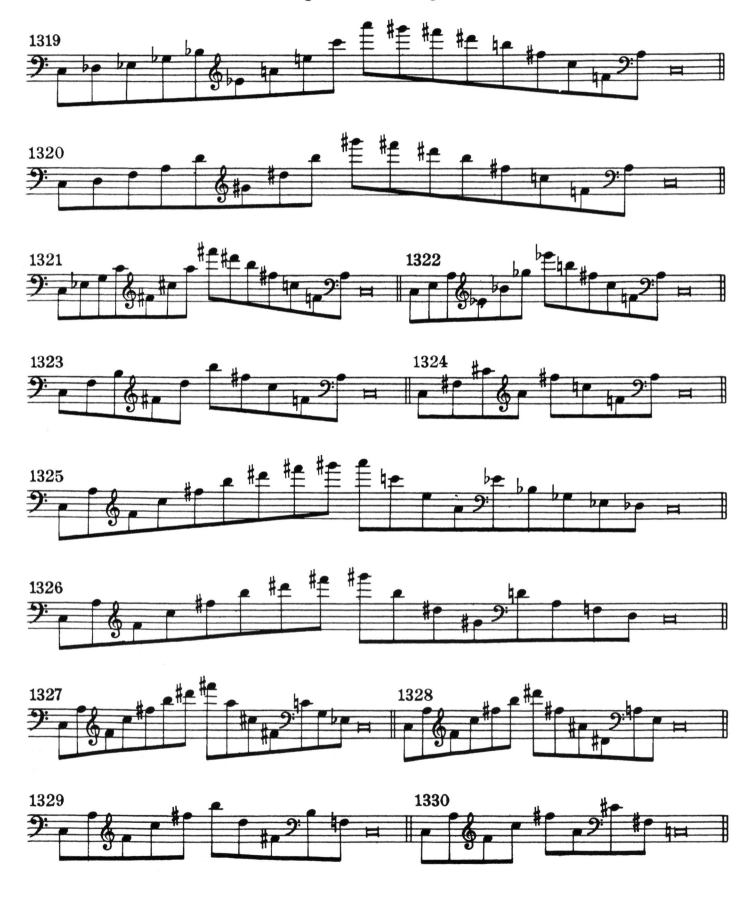

Mirror Interval Progressions

Complementary Scales

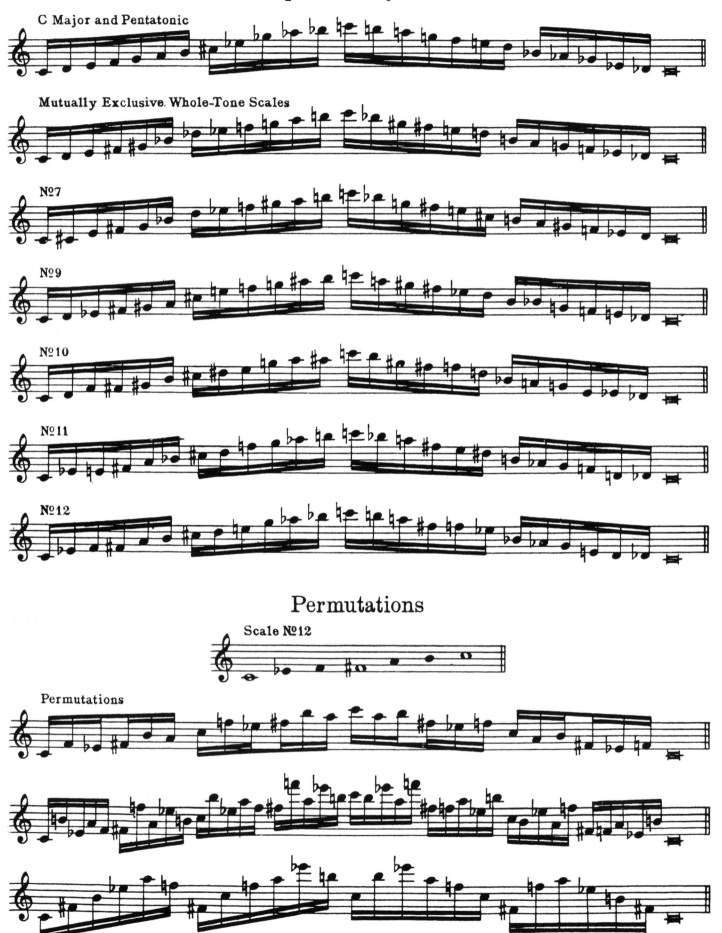

Permutations

Harmonization

Scale №21

Permutations

Pattern №343

Permutations

Pattern №525

Permutations

Pandiatonic Progressions

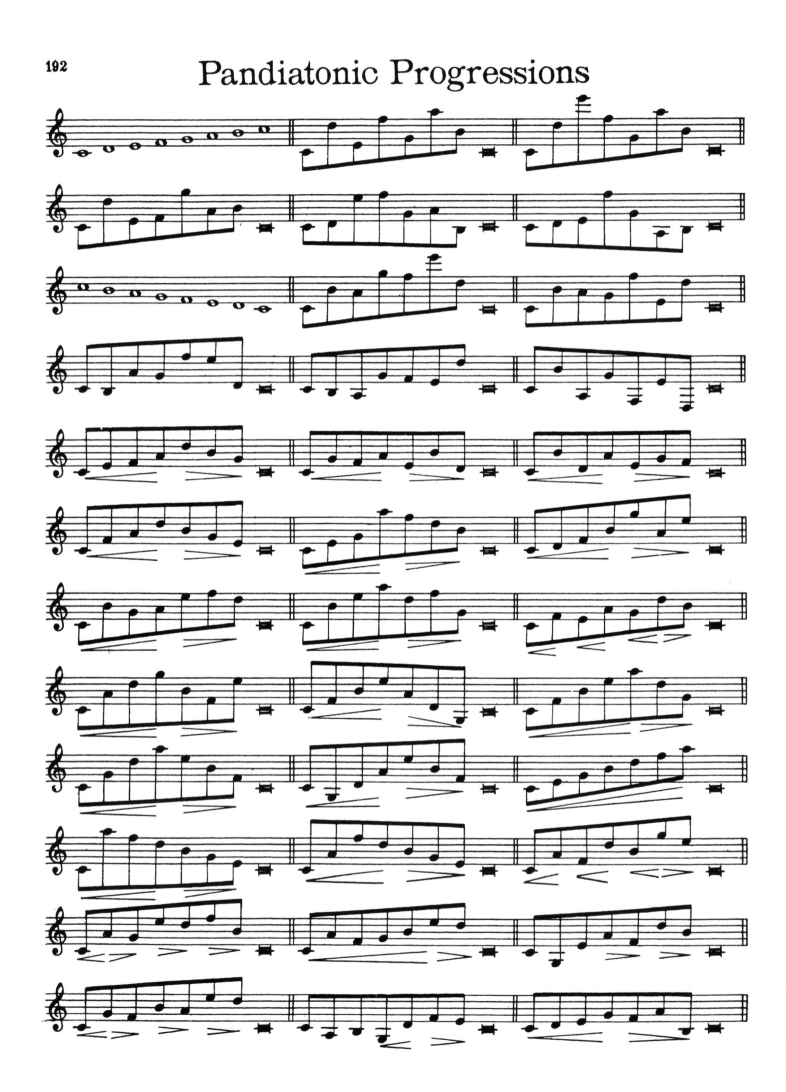

Conjugate Pandiatonic Progressions

Double Notes

Triple Notes

Pandiatonic Counterpoint

Pandiatonic Cadences

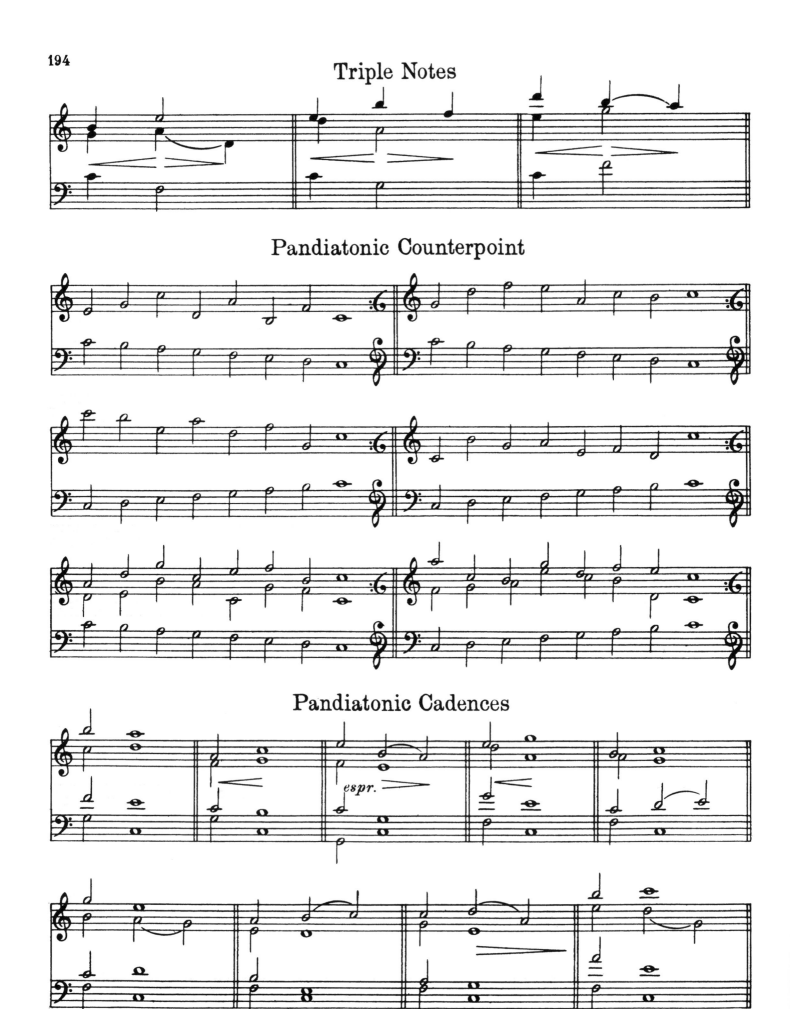

Pandiatonic Harmony in Four Parts

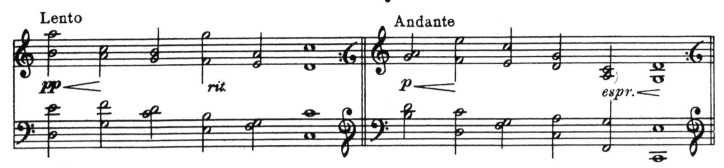

Pandiatonic Harmony in Five Parts

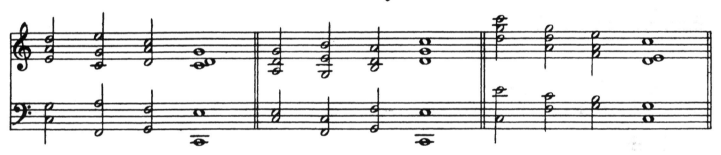

Pandiatonic Harmony in Six Parts

[Roy Harris: *Slumber*]

Pandiatonic Harmony in Seven Parts

Double Notes
Tritone Progression

Numbers in parentheses refer to patterns from which the double notes are derived.

(34)

(35)

(36)

(37)

(38)

(39)

(40)

(41 to 58) *simile*

(59a)　　　　　　　　　(59b)

(60a)　　(60b)　　(61a)　　(61b)　　(62a)

(62b)　　(63a)　　(63b)　　(64a)　　(64b)

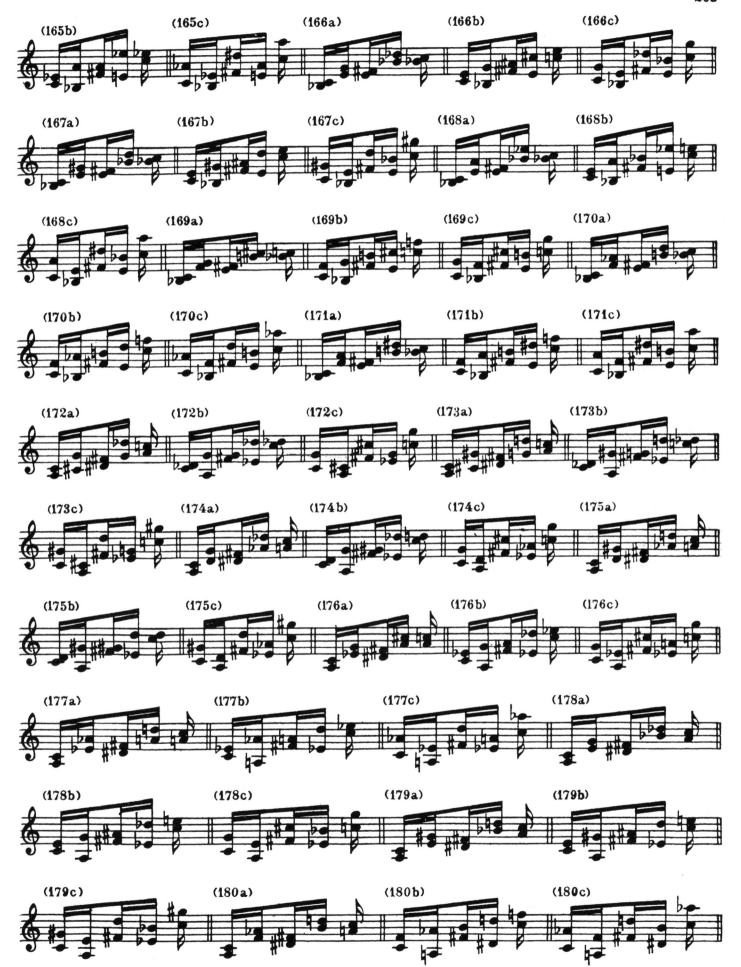

Ditone Progression

(231 to 236) *simile*

Sesquitone Progression

(392a)

(392b)

(392c)

(392d)　(392e)　(392f)

(393a)

(393b)

(393c)

214

Double Notes in Contrary Motion

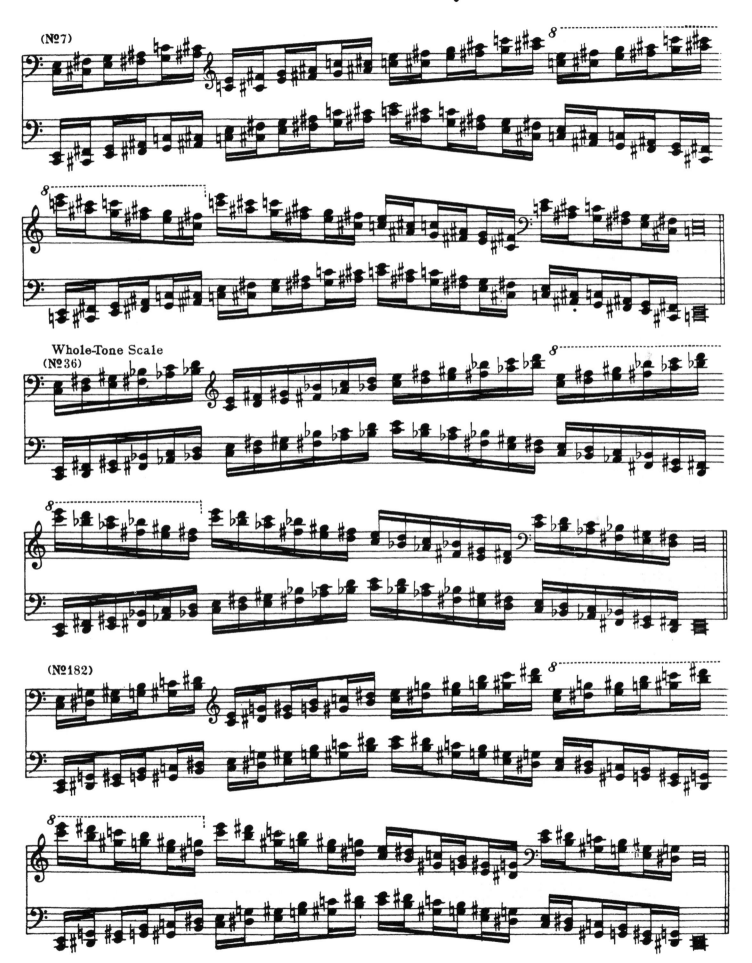

Plural Scales and Arpeggios

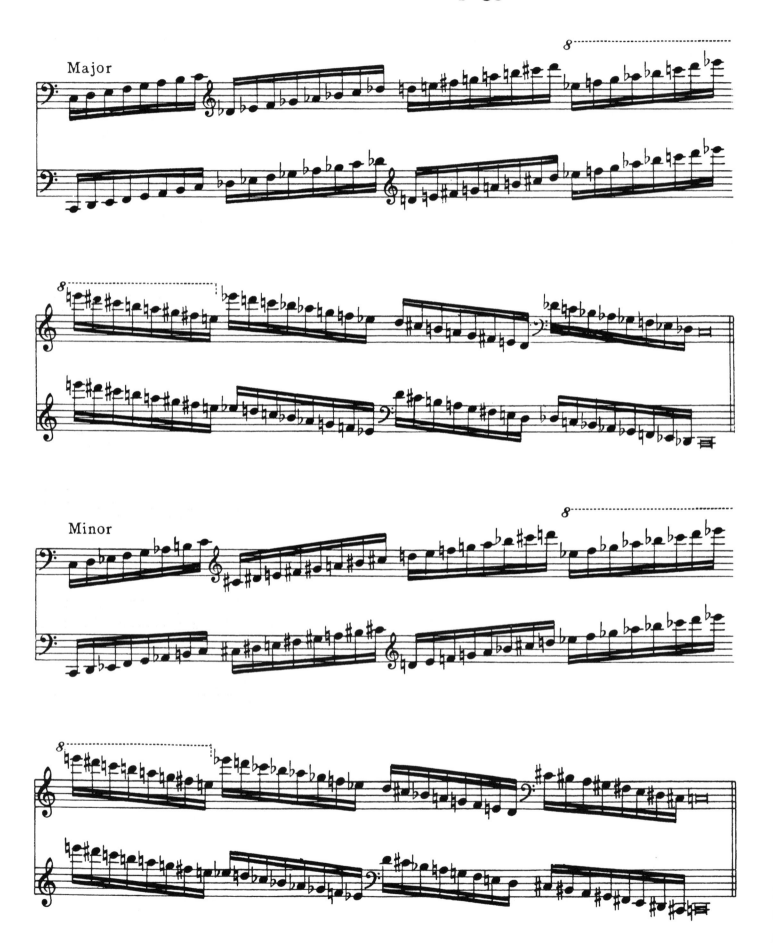

Major

Minor

Augmented

Diminished-Seventh

Polytonal Scales

E♭ Major and C Major

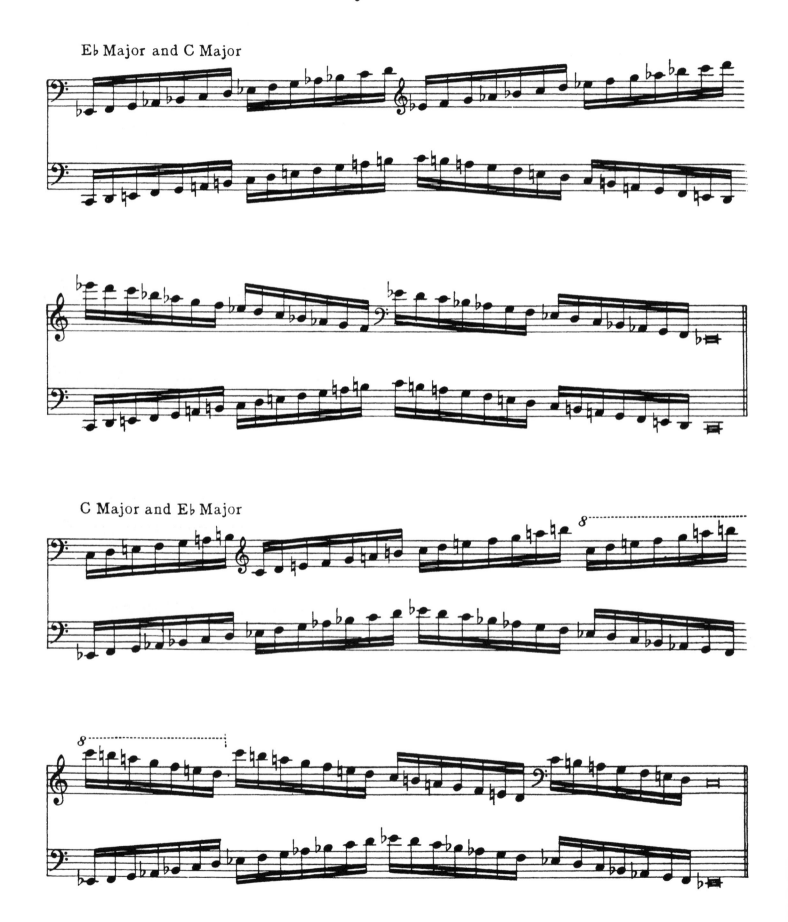

C Major and E♭ Major

E Major and C Major

C Major and E Major

222

A Major and C Major

C Major and A Major

Ab Major and C Major

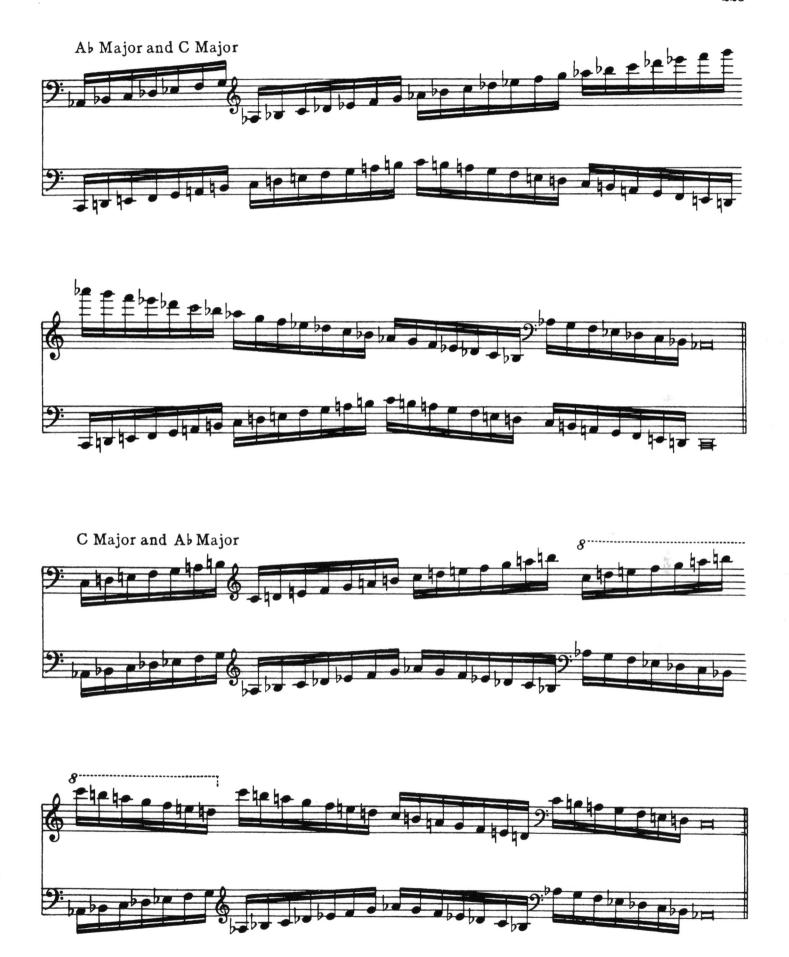

C Major and Ab Major

Polyrhythmic Scales

5: 3

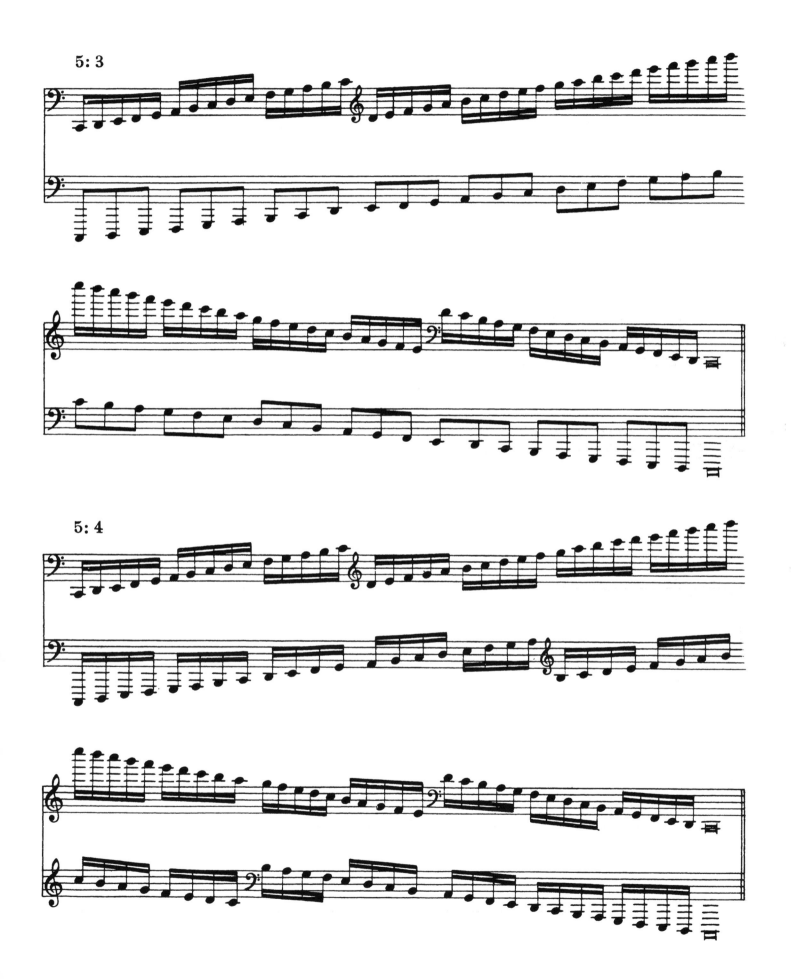

5: 4

Polytonal Polyrhythmic Scales

E Major and C Major; **3: 2**

E Major and C Major; **4: 3**

E Major and C Major; **5: 3**

E Major and C Major; **5: 4**

C Major and E Major; 3: 2

C Major and E Major; 4: 3

C Major and E Major; **5: 3**

C Major and E Major; **5: 4**

Eb Major and C Major; **3: 2**

Eb Major and C Major; **4: 3**

Eb Major and C Major; **5: 3**

Eb Major and C Major; **5: 4**

232

C Major and E♭ Major; 3 : 2

C Major and E♭ Major; 4 : 3

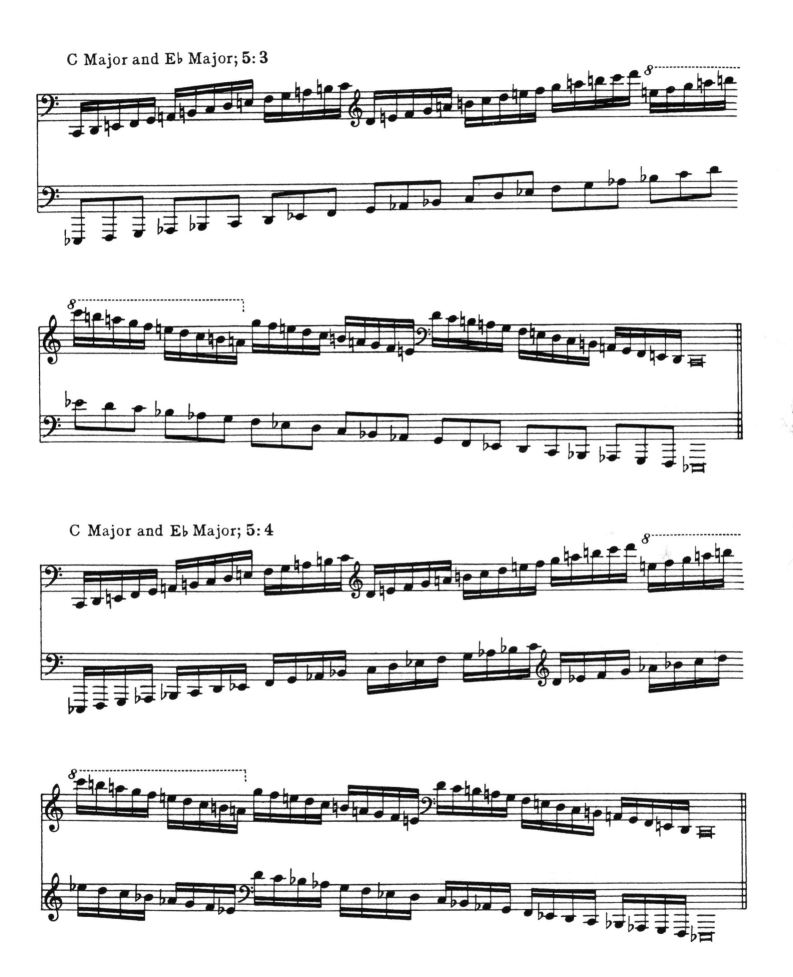

C Major and E♭ Major; 5:3

C Major and E♭ Major; 5:4

Palindromic Canons

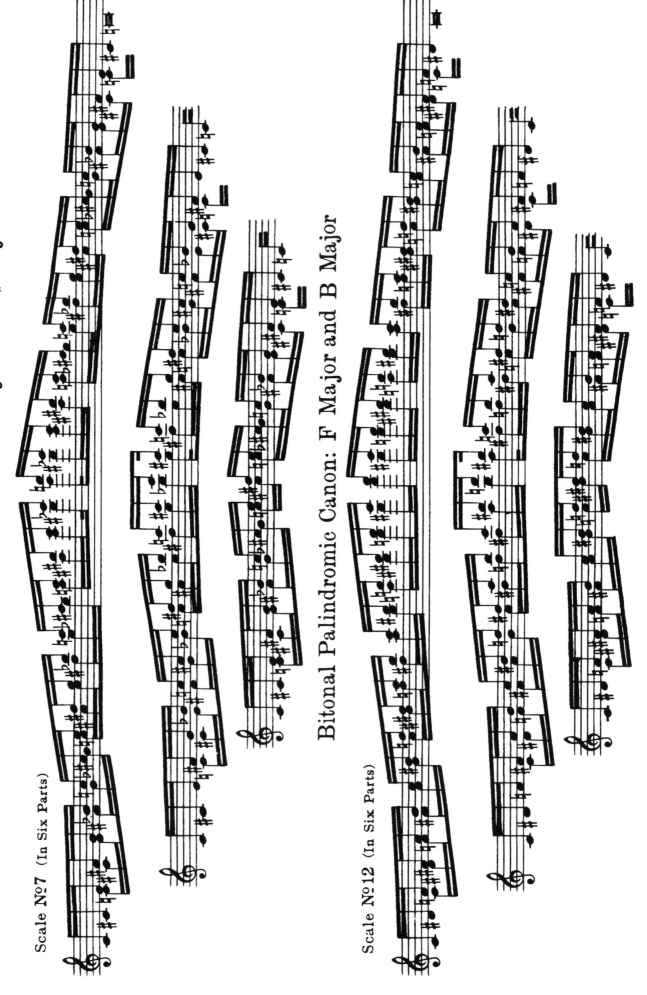

Bitonal Palindromic Canon: C Major and F♯ Major

Scale N⁰7 (In Six Parts)

Bitonal Palindromic Canon: F Major and B Major

Scale N⁰12 (In Six Parts)

Two Palindromic Canons on Pattern 72

In Three Parts
(Alternating Minor and Major Triads)

In Three Parts
(Alternating Major and Minor Triads)

Palindromic Canon on Pattern 141

In Four Parts

235

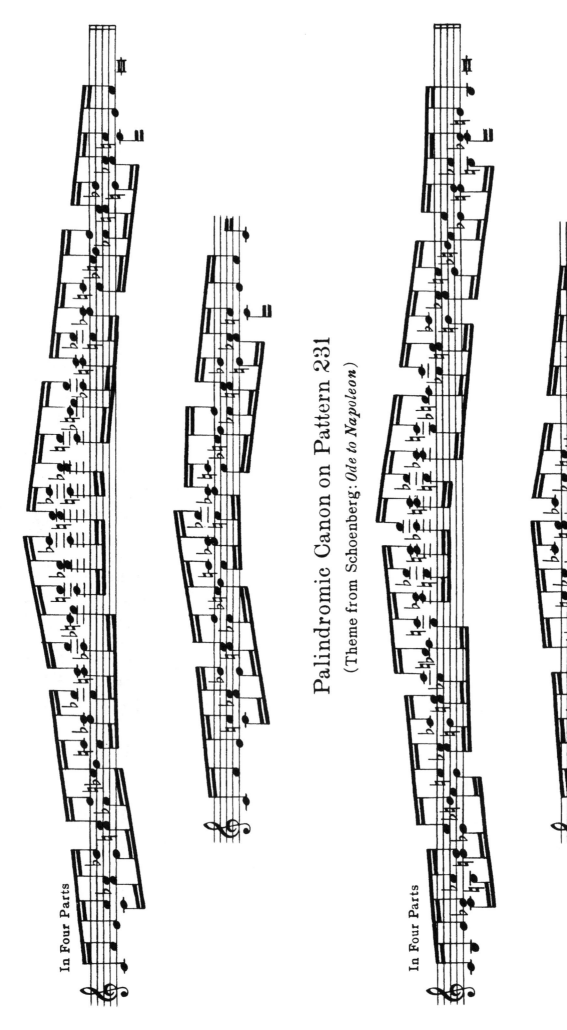

Palindromic Canon on Pattern 186

In Four Parts

Palindromic Canon on Pattern 231

(Theme from Schoenberg: *Ode to Napoleon*)

In Four Parts

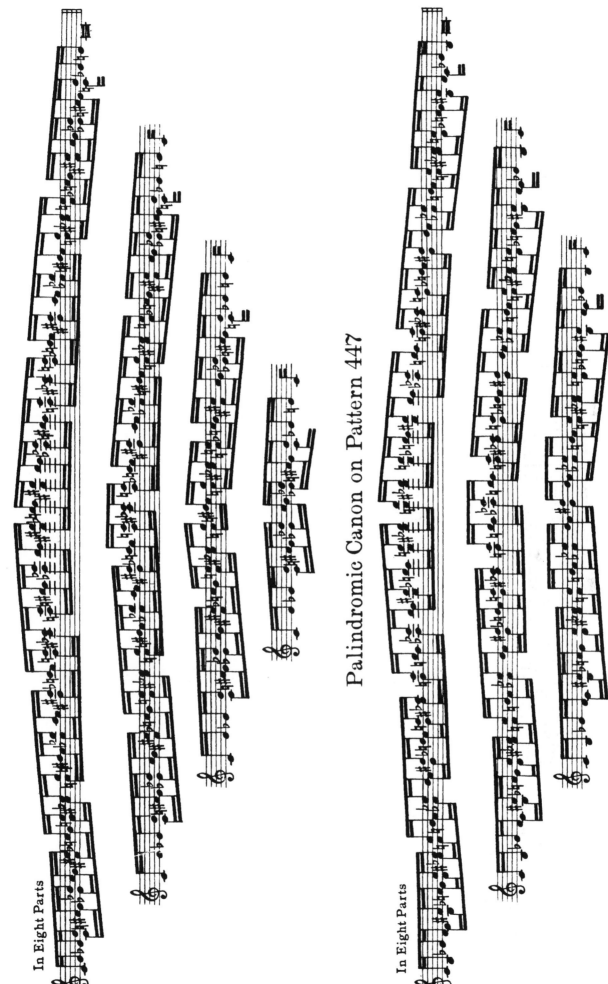

Palindromic Canon on Pattern 394

In Eight Parts

Palindromic Canon on Pattern 447

In Eight Parts

Autochordal Harmonization

240

Harmonization in Major Triads
by Alternation of Octave, Tertian
and Quintan Positions

Melody Line

Octave Position

Tertian Position

Quintan Position

Harmonization in Seventh-Chords,
Ninth-Chords and
Whole-Tone Chords

Melody Line

Whole-Tone Chords

Major Ninth-Chords

Minor Ninth-Chords

Whole-Tone Chords

Dominant Seventh-Chords

Synopsis of Chords

Major
Bitonal Chord

Minor
Bitonal Chord

Whole-Tone
Chord

Prometheus
Chord

(Scriabin)

Quartal
Chord

Containing All Twelve
Chromatic Tones Ar -
ranged in Fourths

Chord
of the Minor 23rd

Containing All Twelve
Chromatic Tones and
Four Mutually Exclusive
Triads

Pandiatonic
Chord

**Containing All Seven
Diatonic Tones**

Pandiatonic
Tone-Cluster

Pentatonic
Tone-Cluster

Pyramid
Chord

**Containing All Twelve
Intervals From an Octave
to a Semitone**

Mother
Chord

**Containing All Twelve
Chromatic Tones and
Eleven Different Inter-
vals**

Grandmother
Chord

**Containing All Twelve
Chromatic Tones and
Eleven Symmetrically
Invertible Intervals**

Master Chords
Tritone Progression
Scales and Patterns 1-180

Master Chords
Ditone Progression
Scales and Patterns 181-391

Master Chords
Sesquitone Progression
Scales and Patterns 392-568